T0120545

"This inspiring book establishes Robert as a bright, new force in presenting the power of faith and the results of commitment!"

Dr. Denis Waitley,
Author of *Seeds of Greatness*

"How about you? If you are: failing in your job... out of a job... having problems with your children or spouse... facing sorrows or adversities... unhappy... this book is for you and all members of your family. It's a masterpiece!"

W. Clement Stone
Founder and Chairman of the Board
Combined International Corporation

"Robert Schuller's sharing of his most personal thoughts through troubled times will be rewarded by the inspiration and help this book will give to others. I know his 'ten steps' will guide many people out of their valleys. His principles of positive thinking will certainly help many through difficult times."

Mary Martin
Award-winning actress

Robert A. Schuller is son of the nation's top-rated televangelist Robert H. Schuller.

Also by Robert A. Schuller:

ROBERT SCHULLER'S LIFE CHANGERS

HOW TO BE AN EXTRAORDINARY
PERSON IN AN ORDINARY WORLD

POWER TO GROW BEYOND YOURSELF

GETTING THROUGH THE GOING-THROUGH STAGE

Robert A. Schuller

BALLANTINE BOOKS • NEW YORK

Library of Congress Catalog Card Number: 86–8770

ISBN 9780345465764

This edition published by arrangement with Thomas Nelson, Inc.

Manufactured in the United States of America

146689836

Psalm 23

The LORD *is* my shepherd;
I shall not want.
He makes me to lie down in green pastures;
He leads me beside the still waters.
He restores my soul;
He leads me in the paths of righteousness
For His name's sake.

Yea, though I walk through the valley of the shadow of death,
I will fear no evil;
For You *are* with me;
Your rod and Your staff, they comfort me.

You prepare a table before me in the presence of my enemies;
You anoint my head with oil;
My cup runs over.
Surely goodness and mercy shall follow me
All the days of my life;
And I will dwell in the house of the LORD
Forever.

Contents

It was Sunday morning, January 8, 1984. I was standing in the pulpit, ready to deliver the morning message to my congregation in the Rancho Capistrano Community Church. Chris Knippers, my assistant, had just finished reading the Twenty-third Psalm. About one hundred fifty people sat in the sanctuary on temporary folding chairs. All their faces were turned toward me in anticipation of my sermon.

Standing at the back of the church, right near the double doors, was Nate Morrison, a stocky, bulldog of a man, whose curly gray hair and wrinkled skin softened the determined set of his jaw. *Dependable Nate*, I thought. *No matter what happens, he will stand with me.* God couldn't have chosen a better man to undergird the everyday work of this church.

Directly in front of the lectern sat Lorraine Fedor. A year earlier when Lorraine had joined the church, I often looked out and saw her eyes filled with tears. Her husband had died suddenly and the loss of his devoted love and support had jolted her, but it had not shaken her trust in God. I knew her heart still felt the pain of loss, but her eyes now smiled up at me.

I bit my lip to stop tears from welling up in my own eyes. Like Lorraine, I, too, was feeling the pain of loss. *But none of these people knows about it*, I reminded myself.

Would today be the day to make the announcement? Next Sunday? Next month? Would I still try to avoid the announcement entirely? I wasn't sure.

I cleared my throat and began my sermon. "Today I am beginning the new series of messages I announced several weeks ago: 'Getting through the Going-through Stage.' Everyone experiences difficult times in life. It may not be a deep valley like the death of a loved one, but everyone is continually faced with challenges. This series of messages is meant to help us solve our problems in positive ways.

"If heart-breaking challenges are facing you this morning, this message is especially for you. Perhaps you're going through a divorce." My voice broke, and I stopped to regain my composure. "Maybe you're facing bankruptcy. Maybe your corporation is reorganizing and your job is threatened. Maybe you're dealing with a delinquent child.

"I don't know what particular problems you are facing this morning, but I want to share with you ten steps that can help you get through your valleys. I, too, have my share of difficulties and I need to apply these principles as much as anyone. In the coming weeks, we will analyze these steps and see how they can help us overcome our challenges.

"You see, we're not dumped in the valley. We're going *through* the valley. The difficult times will not last. As Ethel Waters said, 'God don't sponsor no flops.'" Proclaiming these words loud and clear helped me to repeat the advice to myself.

"The way we get through our valleys is determined by the vehicle we choose. For instance, if we want to travel from Los Angeles to New York City, we can choose many vehicles. We can travel by foot, ride a bike, drive a car, take a train, or fly a 747.

"I have found that we need a vehicle to get through our difficult times. The best vehicle for me was the Twenty-third Psalm. I don't believe there is a chapter in the Bible that speaks more beautifully or more eloquently to someone who is experiencing difficulty.

"Regardless of what you're going through right now, this passage, if applied to your life, can become your vehicle to take you from despair to hope, from sadness to joy, and from failure to success. But like any vehicle it must have fuel. I want to recommend prayer to fuel our vehicle. We will discuss how to pray effectively. We will pray our way through the Twenty-third Psalm and ask God for the guidance we need to get through the going-through stage."

Even though I spoke confidently, I knew there was a chance that the governing body of our church would ask me to take a sabbatical leave or to change churches. I knew, too, that the lay people themselves might feel I had lost credibility. If I couldn't heal my own problems, how could I help them with theirs?

I put these thoughts behind me and continued my sermon. The congregation followed me intently. Their eyes and expressions seemed to say, "That's just how I feel or have felt. I know what it's like. I, too, want to get through the valley."

I ended by quoting a favorite poem of mine, "Footprints in the Sand," which pictures one person's going-through stage.

Now was the time, I knew it. Instead of raising my hands for the benediction, I looked out at the congregation for a moment. Then I began, "In the last few days, God has been carrying me through my own going-through stage. It's a miraculous coincidence that I was preparing these sermons at the same time that my own faith was being tested.

"Two days ago my wife went to an attorney and filed for divorce. Her decision was not made quickly or without counseling; still, it has been devastating for me. I know that we especially need God's love and your support to carry us through our personal going-through stage. Please pray for us."

I raised my hands and spoke the benediction as I had every Sunday for more than two years. "And now may the Lord bless you and keep you. May the Lord make His face to shine upon you and be gracious unto you.... Amen."

Who was I to bless these people? I wondered. My marriage had failed. Would my ministry be able to withstand this defeat? Would the last two years of hard work be destroyed by this failure?

The organist played the introduction to "In Christ There Is No East or West," the traditional congregational response to my message. I turned and walked to one of the three pulpit chairs to the left of the sanctuary.

I buried my face in my hands as the singing echoed through the church. I felt drained. I had done what needed to be be done. I had been honest and straightforward, but it had cost me all my energy and strength for the moment. I sat and wondered about my future. Would the ministry here go on without me? Would it come to an end?

I had first walked into this building in September of 1981. Back then it was nothing more than a large storage building, two hundred feet long and fifty feet wide. It had been donated by John and Donna Crean, founders of Fleetwood Enterprises, one of the world's largest manufacturers of mobile homes and recreational vehicles. The Creans had been using it to house their personal collection of automobiles and motor homes. Large, sliding metal doors had covered the front and back ends of the building, as well as the left wall, so that semi-trucks could drive through, and a four-thousand-pound hoist, almost as long as the building itself, had hung from the ceiling.

I looked about me on this Sunday morning and thought of all the changes we had made. The steel doors on the left side of the building had been replaced by a series of huge, plate-glass windows. They made the outside hills and pines and scrub grass seem like a natural part of the sanctuary. At the front we had installed a huge stained-glass window depicting the Good Shepherd and his sheep. Two smaller windows continued the pastoral scene of grazing lambs. At this time of year the windows usually caught the sun just right to illuminate the scene majestically during our 11:00 A.M. service.

Once established, the church had grown quickly. Some people initially came because of the lovely setting. Others came because I was the son of Dr. Robert H. Schuller, the pastor of the Crystal Cathedral, and they wanted to see if I had the same charisma my father had. Still others came because we had converted the large Crean family home into a retreat complex called Rancho Capistrano Renewal Center. I preached with a sincere and caring heart and soon more than two hundred people decided to join the church.

I became very involved in my work. There was remodeling to consider, fund-raising to plan for, and church growth to project. There were new families to visit, sermons to prepare, hospital calls to make, and board meetings to conduct. Through it all, I assumed that my wife, Linda, and I were of one mind in all that I was doing. After all, this was our ministry and our future. But that was a costly assumption on my part.

My parents had been happily married for more than three decades. Mom had been Dad's right arm through times both lean and prosperous. As newlyweds they had hitched a U-Haul trailer to their beat-up old station wagon and had pulled Mom's portable organ with them from church to church, preaching, witnessing, and singing. They hadn't had one extra nickle to spend in those days, but they were crazy in love and completely committed to their goal of one day building a large church to the glory of God.

I had always imagined that when I got married my wife would be just as supportive as Mom. I was even more convinced of this after I fell in love with Linda, a fine Christian girl whom I had known since we were teenagers singing in the choir of my father's church. We got engaged when I was a college sophomore and married very young. We probably should have waited, but I felt that our love for each other was strong enough to carry us "'til death do us part."

But Linda wasn't my mother. And I wasn't my father. Whereas my mother had been completely loyal and supportive of my father, Linda wanted to go her own way. Similarly, whereas my father had included my mother in all of his travels, his church services, and his planning sessions, I had usually worked independently of Linda. I had wanted her to become more involved in the church but her desires and dreams carried her in a different direction, and we had become more and more like strangers. Ours was not a harmonious union.

As this became more obvious, I became even more involved in the long-range plans for Rancho Capistrano. The future potential for the church and the renewal center, of which I was now president, sent my imagination into over-drive. These ninety-seven acres had originally been part of a four-thousand-acre tract given to Father Junipero Serra by King Charles II of Spain in 1776 so that the priest could establish the mission at San Juan Capistrano.

More recently, my father and I had considered it the perfect site to establish the first of what we hoped would one day be a nationwide network of more than twenty family retreat centers. We had already begun a ten-suite addition to John and Donna Crean's ranch home. I dreamed, too, of establishing a holistic resource center associated with the church which would meet people's mental, physical, and spiritual needs.

I also had some goals for our church building—a plush, blue carpet to cover the bare floors, and carved wooden pews instead of the temporary rows of folding chairs.

Now I wondered if any of these goals would be reached. How would the consistory, the governing body of our church, respond to my divorce? Whatever the local congregation and the national church decided, I still had to deal with my own conscience. Could I continue to serve as a minister?

One particular passage of Scripture was all too familiar to me: "A bishop [minister] then must be blameless, the husband of one wife . . . one who rules his own house well . . . for if a man does not know how to rule his own house, how will be take care of the church of God?"[1]

Because of this passage I felt my ministry might be over. How could I minister to my congregation when I had not ruled my own house well? My wife had filed for a divorce. She believed so strongly that our relationship was over, even months of counseling had not helped us reconcile our differences.

Additionally, I felt I could never be married again. Another passage of Scripture kept running through my mind: "And I say to you, whoever divorces his wife, except for sexual immorality, and marries another, commits adultery; and whoever marries her who is divorced commits adultery."[2]

During the week after the announcement, I told my father about my thoughts. I have rarely seen him cry, but the tears streamed down his face that day.

He mentioned our good friend Steve McWhorter, rector of St. Paul's Episcopal Church of Walnut Creek, California. Steve had preached at the Crystal Cathedral and shared the story of how his ministry had nearly ended in 1971. At that time, he was rector of the Church of the Redeemer in Pittsburgh, Pennsylvania. He had been married two years when his marriage fell apart.

"Steve was devastated," my father reminded me. "He told me he had never felt so depressed and hollow and lonely in his whole life. The feelings you are feeling, Robert, are only natural." Dad paused for a moment to emphasize his point. Then he went on. "The day his wife left, Steve drove her to the airport. He stopped at the home of his bishop on the way home, who invited Steve in and fixed them some soft drinks. They talked and Steve poured out his soul to him. Steve admitted he was confused, that he didn't know what to do. He wasn't sure whether or not he could maintain his ministry.

"The bishop let Steve finish his story, then said, 'There are two things you can do, Steve: you can fulfill the ministry and call God has given you, or you can quit and walk away. It's that simple.'

"Steve told me how lonely he felt that first weekend by himself as he thought about what his bishop had said. Sunday morning he rose early and went to his church to preach the eight o'clock service. There, on the front row, seated right at the center were his bishop and his wife. It was their way of saying they loved and cared for Steve and would stand by him. That faith and encouragement enabled him to get through his going-through stage."

Dad looked directly at me and said very slowly, "You can continue on, just as Steve did. Your congregation will support you. Just allow God to work in your life."

At that moment I had a hard time believing my father. But in the days and weeks and months ahead, he kept repeating the principles of positive thinking to me, and God worked in my life to move me through the going-through stage.

Getting through the valley is extremely difficult, *but it is not impossible*. I found ten steps that helped me make this journey successfully. I'd like to share these steps with you in the coming chapters. You, too, can get through the valley and come out on top.

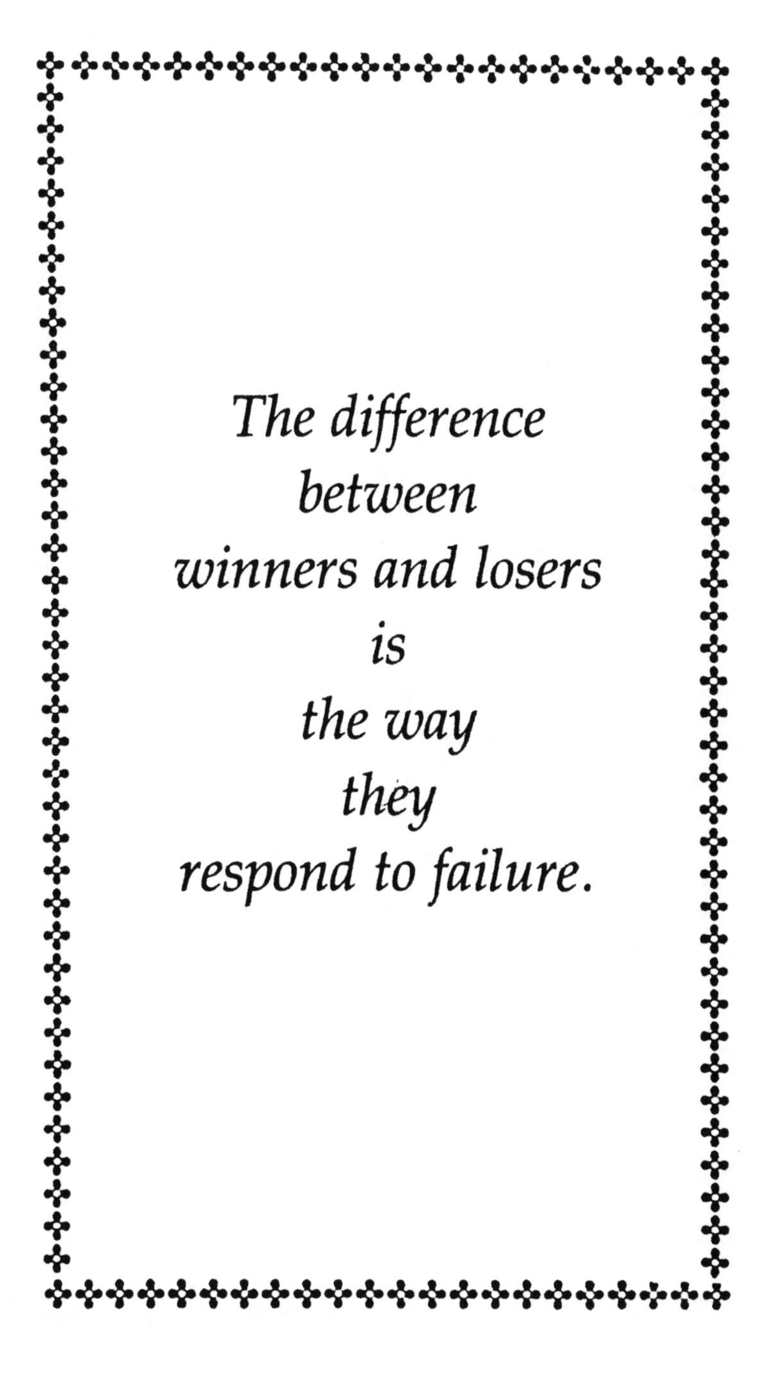
*The difference
between
winners and losers
is
the way
they
respond to failure.*

STEP ONE

✥ ✥ ✥

Look at Your Life Positively.

"The Lord is my shepherd. I shall not want."

In the weeks after my announcement to the congregation, I realized that in order to get through the valley I had to evaluate where I was before I could decide where I was going. If I had been dumped in the middle of the Sahara Desert and didn't know where I was, I wouldn't have had much chance of finding my way home. Similarly, I couldn't get through the going-through stage if I didn't first discover where I was starting from emotionally and spiritually. So, the first step in getting through the going-through stage is to take a positive look at your life. Answer two bold questions constructively:

- Where am I?
- Where am I going?

Where Am I?

In my case, I began by admitting that my marriage was over. My great-uncle, a missionary to China, and my father were clergymen, and divorce had always been totally unacceptable to our family's conservative theology. But I knew God would forgive me, for grace is a gift from God and not something we earn through good works. I reminded myself of verses such as, "He's quick to forgive" and "He is faithful and just to forgive us our sins."[1]

If you, too, have fallen short in one area of your life, God will forgive you. Never forget that. His mercy is perpetual, boundless, infinite.

After coming to terms with the fact that my marriage was over, I next had to confront the feelings that were whirling inside me. I was hurt, I was angry, I was defensive. I felt that Linda had rejected me. That wounded my pride.

I looked back over the recent years and realized that I'd felt rejected several other times, too. I'd held on and God had pulled me through, but each instance had been painful. One of the ways I keep going when my troubles seem to be overwhelming is to remember how God has helped me through other difficult times, so I began to review my life and remember the times God had turned impossibilities into possibilities.

I had graduated from Fuller Theological Seminary in Pasadena and been ordained into Christian ministry at the Crystal Cathedral in September of 1980. That week I began to work for my dad as the minister of evangelism, whose job description was "to recruit, motivate, and inspire lay persons to be lay ministers of evangelism."

After six months, I began to feel restless. I had walked into a ministry that had been prepared for me. Instead of beginning with nothing, as my dad had done, I had been given a spacious and modern office on one of the top floors of the Cathedral's Tower of Hope. Everyone knew whose son I was. No one questioned my plans or directives. Where was the challenge? I felt coddled.

I called my father's secretary and asked her to clear a day on the calendar for Dad and me to have a leisurely lunch together. The next week we went to a nearby restaurant and sequestered ourselves in a corner booth.

After we ordered lunch, I told Dad about the weekend retreat the evangelism committee had just sponsored. Four years earlier, when I had served as an intern at the Crystal Cathedral, I had helped to start a small group movement. We had begun with ten groups of eight to thirty members, each meeting informally in homes for Bible study and prayer. Now one hundred groups met each week, and the leaders of each group went away to a camp in the mountains three times a year to plan the next months of Bible study. These retreats were always a time of spiritual enrichment and personal evaluation for everyone attending, including me.

"I did some evaluating myself, Dad," I admitted. "I believe the Lord is calling me to a preaching ministry, and I'm really torn about what to do. There's really no opportunity for me to preach Sunday after Sunday at the cathedral, and I can't develop as a preacher if I'm not under that continual pressure to prepare a weekly sermon."

Dad finished his last bite of salad and pushed the plate away. "You could preach at the eight o'clock Sunday morning service," he suggested.

"I'm not sure that would be a true test of my ability. We both know that one of the best ways to test a preacher's skill is to watch the attendance and see if it grows. That congregation has already been developed, and the people are already dedicated to the church."

"What about Sunday nights?"

"Well, to begin with, the congregation's just as devoted," I reminded him. "But I also sense a national trend away from attending Sunday evening services. We could be hit by that in the future. Then the effect would be just the opposite. I could be doing a great job, but the attendance would be going down because of this trend.

"Actually, Dad, I really feel that God is calling me to start a new ministry someplace, just as you did twenty-six years ago. I don't know when. I don't know where. I do know that I want to start with nothing and build it from there."

"But, Robert, it's not like it used to be," he replied immediately. "Starting churches is a costly and time-consuming undertaking.

"Why don't you pray about it some more," he suggested. "You could always stay with the Crystal Cathedral two or three more years. Learn how we operate. Test your skills by developing new outreach projects right within our ministry."

Dad then dropped the subject of my leaving. We spent the rest of our lunchtime discussing a variety of matters related to our work at the Crystal Cathedral. All during our discussion, however, I kept thinking about my need to move on. I knew that my father had great wisdom and that I should probably heed his advice, but I left that luncheon with my mind still not made up.

A few days later, on the Tuesday of Holy Week in

1981, we had a church board meeting. This was an unusual meeting because there was no agenda. Dad announced, "Today I would like all of us to share something that is happening in our lives. It might be something you'd like us to pray about or a decision you'd like us to consider with you."

I listened as other members of the board began sharing their thoughts and feelings. *Does Dad want me to tell the board about my decision?* I wondered. *Does he want me to announce my resignation?*

I still wasn't sure what I should say when Dad asked me, "What is new and exciting in your life?"

At first I talked about the prayer ministry I had begun at the Crystal Cathedral. Prayer partners were manning the chapel of the "Hour of Power" twenty-four hours a day to pray for the thousands of requests we received each week. Launching this new program had been quite an undertaking and I was proud of it.

"Is there anything else?" my father asked, looking directly into my eyes.

I misinterpreted his glance to mean: "Share if you dare." This seemed to be the moment to make my feelings public. My lips started to quiver as I began to speak. "I feel that God is leading me to start a new ministry—someplace, somewhere, sometime, somehow. I do not know when. I do not know where. I do not know how." My voice broke with emotion. "I just know that God is leading me to start a new church." I felt tears welling up in my eyes, so I excused myself. I left the room and regained my composure.

When I returned several minutes later, it was obvious that Dad was shocked by my announcement. The ball was in my court, so I explained. "I want to be a great preacher. I don't believe I'll ever be able to be the man God wants me to be unless I stretch myself to grow. I've been praying a long time, and I really believe God wants me to get out and start my own church from scratch the way Dad did."

I could feel my eyes filling with tears again. The significance of what I had just said swept over me. I had been only six months old when Dad began his ministry. I could remember vividly the years as a youngster when Mom kept me busy with coloring books, while Dad stood on top of the refreshment booth of a drive-in movie theater and preached to rows of cars on Sunday mornings. When I was sick, I had to stay in my pajamas and sleep in the car because my parents couldn't afford a sitter. Later when the first building—a little stained-glass chapel—was built on two acres of land in Garden Grove, I began standing with my father, among the folds of his robe. When Dad shook hands with the people after the service, my small hand protruded from his side seeking an additional handshake.

When I was six, I helped Dad plant the first trees in front of his drive-in church. I spent a couple of Saturdays each spring after that planting more one-gallon cypress trees, only four feet tall, around the edge of the property. Now there were two-hundred pine, cypress, and eucalyptus trees on the cathedral property and the cypress trees were thirty feet tall.

Over the years our entire family—my four sisters and I and my mom and dad—had worked together to build Dad's church. We were all involved in our current ministry, the three-thousand-seat cathedral with its ten thousand members, the youth programs, the helping hand to the needy in our community, the internationally televised "Hour of Power" with its four million viewers, and the publication of our monthly magazine, books, and tapes. The Crystal Cathedral was a family venture.

Now I was leaving the ministry. The significance of this act escaped no one around the table. I was surrendering my life to God.

I fielded a variety of questions from the board members. I was honest in saying that I did not know yet where God would lead me. Then I asked for the guidance of the Holy Spirit and the approval of the board. All twelve stood, linked arms, and prayed for me. Afterward they embraced me and wished me well.

Still, I could see concern in my father's eyes. He was never one to hold back progress or to thwart the moving of the Holy Spirit, but he was concerned over the timing of my decision. Was I acting prematurely?

Before I left the room, Dad cornered me. "What's on your calendar for tomorrow?" he asked.

"I have to drive to San Diego for a dental appointment," I said. "But it will only take a half hour. We could have lunch together afterward."

"Fine," said Dad, "I'll ride along with you. We can spend the time discussing your future plans."

I was glad that Dad was able to clear his calendar to be with me. The simple fact was, I *wanted* to be with my father.

The ninety-mile drive south on Interstate 5 is a pleasant drive along the beautiful coast of California. My father and I had a lot of time to discuss my decision. He asked practical questions like, "How do you expect to buy the land?"

"When I started my church," he said, "we were able to buy land for six thousand dollars an acre. Today it's more like $60,000 to $600,000 an acre, and even then there isn't much vacant land to be bought."

As he explained this economic reality we were passing the grand old estate of Rancho Capistrano, ninety-seven gorgeous acres of cultivated and virgin land owned by John and Donna Crean, the industrialists who had donated the first million-dollar gift to the Crystal Cathedral. I looked over at the Creans' oasis of lush, green palm and olive trees, which covered the rise leading up to the main house. A low, white stucco wall topped with hundreds of red bougainvillea bore the brick inscription: *Rancho Capistrano*. Above that and to the left, an American flag flew in the center of the courtyard of the main house.

I felt the Holy Spirit speaking to me as I never had before. I pointed to the ranch and said, "Dad, that's where I am going to build my church." I did not say, "I would *like* to build my church there," or "*Maybe* I could build my church there." There were no ifs, ands, or buts. I simply said, "That's where *I am going to build* my church."

As Dad turned to look at that impressive hillside, I added, "I believe it might be possible to get a gift of ten acres of that land for a church."

My father began to get excited. "Well, Robert," he said, "if you're willing to ask John Crean for ten acres of land, why not ask him for twenty?"

"Well, Dad, if I'm going to ask for twenty, I might as well ask for forty," I said.

By the time we arrived in San Diego, we had decided I would ask John Crean to donate all ninety-seven acres of Rancho Capistrano to our ministry so I could begin a dynamic new church in southern Orange County and Dad would begin a retreat center for married couples, emotionally drained ministers, and persons dealing with problems of alcoholism. My father's positive thinking made mountains seem like mole hills.

The next day I met with John Crean at his forty-acre assembly plant in Riverside where he manufactures hundreds of recreational vehicles every year. It was Maundy Thursday of 1981, three days before Easter and five years exactly from the day Dad had asked him for the million-dollar gift to the Crystal Cathedral.

Knowing he was a busy man, I avoided small talk and went straight to the subject of our meeting. "John," I said, "I believe God has called me to start a dynamic new church in San Juan Capistrano." I went on to describe my plans for the church. Then I asked, "Will you donate your ranch to me so we can do this?"

John Crean put his hands behind his head, leaned back in the swivel chair behind his desk, and said, "Donna and I have been wondering for a long time what we would do with Rancho Capistrano. Just last night we signed the papers deeding the entire property to another Christian organization."

I was shocked. So close and yet so far. After I recovered my composure, I said, "John, is it possible for you to carve out a ten-acre parcel for a church?"

"No, Robert, the entire gift is in concrete. The transaction has been made. I'm afraid it's out of my control." He went on to explain a few of the particulars of the gift and then suggested that we go out for lunch.

Once we were seated in the restaurant and had ordered our meals, I began to play the possibility thinker's game. "John, in order for me to build a church, I need at least ten acres of land. Since land averages nearly $250,000 an acre, that would be $2½ million, which is an enormous hurdle for a small church to overcome."

I will never forget what John said to me at that moment. "Start with nothing, Robert. Go out there and form a congregation. The land will come from the people. In fact, you might want to do what your dad did thirty years ago—start your church in a drive-in theater. There's a theater in San Juan Capistrano, the Mission Theater. Maybe you could work out an arrangement with them so you could hold services there."

The idea was a good one. A few weeks later I went to see John Crean's son, Johnny, at his Alpha Leisure Mobile Trailer plant in Chino. He was interested in joining the new church and promised to be on the steering committee. In the next months Johnny helped me contract office space in the Birtcher Plaza; he had caught my dream and was helping to make it a reality. He also knew I still felt there was no better site for the new church than Rancho Capistrano. Sometimes I wonder if Johnny invited me to the special Fourth of July birthday party for his dad so I would see the finality of their gift to the other Christian organization.

"We're going to announce Dad's gift of the ranch during the party," Johnny told me. "It will be a very special day."

Johnny knew I had been raised with the philosophy of possibility thinking. "Nothing is impossible," my father had preached to me as frequently as he had to his congregation. Johnny Crean knew I still had not given up my impossible dream that someday my church would be located on their ranch. And he was right.

That Fourth of July, I drove up the long driveway that wound into the ranch. What a contrast it presented to the many places I was now considering as possible church sites: a drive-in, a shopping center, schools—all concrete, utilitarian buildings. No one could drive into the ranch without being overwhelmed by the beauty and serenity of that oasis. The lush, green trees and bushes surrounding the house looked even richer alongside the brown, rolling hills dotted with scrub grass that surrounded the property. Rancho Capistrano was truly a desert in bloom.

The party was held on the lawn behind the ranch house. People were chatting in small groups and enjoying the hors d'oeuvres spread out on a huge buffet table when I arrived. Half an hour later, Johnny Crean asked everyone to gather around the patio for an announcement.

"Today, as part of my father's birthday celebration, I am pleased to make a very special announcement," he began. He went on to describe a couple of incidents from his childhood on the ranch. He said Rancho Capistrano had meant a great deal to him and his family. They would never want it to be developed into residential condominiums, the way much of the adjacent land would be. He motioned toward the north to lands that had already been sold to developers.

"We have always dreamed that this ranch would be used as a retreat center," he said, "so we've decided to give the ranch to a Christian organization. Members of this church will be moving into the ranch next week. I'd like to introduce the men to you today."

I watched the representatives of the organization come forward and saw Johnny hand them a piece of paper, which I assumed was the deed to the ranch. As I saw them receive the gift I couldn't help thinking, *This will never work.* I knew the amount of work required to make the ranch all that it should be, and I knew that this group did not have the resources to make these changes. I still felt the ranch would be given to the Robert Schuller Ministries.

But I also knew that the Creans felt I was too young, too immature, too inefficient to be able to handle the project. Looking back on that day now, several years later, I realize they were probably right. I probably didn't have the resources at my disposal to make it work. Not alone.

During the month of August I contacted people I knew in southern Orange County and others whose names were on the "Hour of Power" mailing list. Johnny Crean and his wife and other couples on the steering committee invited their friends to open houses to meet me and hear my dreams for the new church.

I also contacted the theater and negotiated a contract to rent its facility every Sunday morning. I bought advertising space in the local paper and announced a beginning service for September 21. Everything was ready to go. All I needed was a Use Permit.

Days before we were to hold our first service, the city council met and denied our permit. "It will cause traffic problems at the intersection," they said. *How could this happen now*? I wondered.

We had already advertised the first service, and we knew that people would be coming. Since there was no time to cancel, I decided to turn a negative into a positive. That Sunday, I stood with Nate Morrison and other helpers at the drive-in and gave out handouts about our new church. We explained what had happened, assured the people that the church would exist in spite of this setback, and asked them to write down their names and addresses so we could notify them of the next service. That list of fifteen people became the first membership roster of Capistrano Community Church.

My first proposal had been rejected by John Crean. My second proposal had been rejected by the San Juan Capistrano City Council. On Monday I approached the Mission Viejo Mall Shopping Center. Could we hold services before the mall opened on Sunday? Again the answer was no. I tried every grammar school and high school in the area. Most of these facilities were already being used by churches. Again my proposal was rejected.

Finally, I sat alone in my office and had a talk with myself. I re-evaluated my decision.

Did I, personally, feel ready to take on a new ministry?

Yes!

Did I honestly feel that God was calling me to do a great work?

Yes!

Did the people of the San Juan Capistrano area want me to help establish a new church for them?

Yes!

Did I really believe the Holy Spirit had spoken to me about building a church at Rancho Capistrano?

Yes!

Had God provided an alternative place for me to build a church?

No!

Therefore, God must have wanted me to build a church at Rancho Capistrano, but for some reason the time had not been right yet.

I lowered my head in prayer. "Lord, I yield my work to you and I put my trust in your wisdom and perfect timing. When you say the time is right, I'll hear and act."

I could only think of one other facility large enough to hold a church meeting: Saddleback Community College. I went to see the president of the college. He told me he admired the work the Crystal Cathedral was doing in California and asked how he could help. I didn't delay in asking him for use of his college gym on Sundays.

For the first time since I'd announced my intention eight months before, the answer was yes. We could hold our services in the gymnasium if we covered the entire floor with a huge canvas tarp to prevent scuffing and if we set our equipment up immediatly before the service and put it away immediately afterward. We could also rent some of the classrooms for nursery and Sunday school classes.

Again Nate Morrison came to my aid. He organized a group he called the "crew of the faithful," seven men who, in the hour before the service, pulled the canvas over the basketball court, set up at least two-hundred chairs, hauled a piano and an organ, a pulpit, and the sound equipment out of a storage closet and set them up for the service, all by 9:30 A.M.

On November 1, 1981, we held our first service in Saddleback College, and I began the fastest declining church in the history of mankind. That first Sunday we had 450 people. I recognized most of them. They were all friends from the Crystal Cathedral who had come to launch the infant church. The next Sunday many of the same people came back. Three weeks later, however, I stood in the pulpit and looked out upon a crowd of 85 strangers and a room filled with hundreds of empty chairs. This, I realized, was the true core of my new church. Well, fine! I would build from there.

The gym was neither heated nor air-conditioned. All winter the people wore heavy coats. All that summer one single fan moved the warm air. Still the "crew of the faithful" prepared the church by 9:30 A.M. each Sunday and by 7:30 P.M. each Friday for our family night services.

One Sunday we decided to hang banners from the steel girders to make the gym more festive. The tallest member of that faithful crew tied the end of a long string around his tennis shoe and threw it up into the air, just short of the girder. A second try and the shoe hit the girder. The third try was a winner. He tied the other end of the string to the yellow banner proclaiming "Bloom Where You Are Planted" and hung it behind the pulpit. The next Sunday the same tall member of the seven attempted this feat again. This time the tennis shoe went up above the girder and landed on the top. As far as I know it's still there.

In September of 1982 Donna and John Crean asked my dad and mom to come to the ranch late one afternoon. They had some important news: the other Christian organization had not returned the contract for the ranch, signed and notarized, in the allotted six months. Crean had decided to give the ranch to the Robert Schuller Ministries and "The Hour of Power." My parents were overjoyed by this wonderful news.

As they discussed the details, Dad said, "John, you know this is an answer to prayer. It all started when my son, in prayer, asked for a place to start his church."

At that point, Crean interrupted. "Bob, I am giving this to you for a retreat center and for your church purposes. It is not for young Robert. He has to earn his own way. He has to experience his own struggles. It is my dream that this will be a retreat center, not just another church."

You can imagine how I felt when my dad repeated the conversation to me. I was pleased for my father. His dream had come true. Possibility thinking had worked again—for him. But my church was left out in the cold with no place to go. For the first time since I had begun my ministry in San Juan I wondered if I would ever be able to find property for the new church.

My fears became a reality in the spring of 1983. Without warning we received a notice from the college that we would no longer be able to hold services in its facilities.

"But we have no place to go," I protested. The answer remained a definite no. This left me facing the threat I had feared from the very beginning: what if I spent years forming a congregation and suddenly we were thrown out with no place to go? How could a young church afford to buy land?

I investigated the same facilities I had contacted eighteen months before. Again and again the answer was no. Finally I had no other option but to make an appointment with John Crean to ask if he would reconsider and allow our church to hold services in the old warehouse on Rancho Capistrano.

John didn't give me a direct answer. "I'll think about it," he said. "I'm going fishing with your dad this weekend. We're going to talk about his plans for developing the ranch. Maybe we can discuss it then."

As my dad and John Crean cruised the Pacific together that weekend, fishing for marlin, John Crean told my father, "You know, I am very impressed with the job young Robert has done. My son has been going to his church. He has joined it. Did you know that?" He turned to look at Dad. "A lot has happened during the last year. Young Robert has proven himself. If he'd like to use the old barn at the other end of the property, make it into a little chapel, and have his church meet there, I think that might work out all right."

At last my joy was complete. *My* goal had been reached. The impossible dream had become a reality.

Whenever I feel low, I think back to that triumphant time. Good memories *do* help us to move ahead when times are tough.

Remembering how God has guided you through a difficult time is one way to help you get through the going-through stage. Your prayer should be, "Guide me, Lord. Guide me again, as you did before."

This secret of "remembering" is time-tested. What did Moses say to the Israelites as he prepared them to conquer the Promised Land? "Remember the days of old. . . . for the LORD's portion is His people; Jacob is the place of His inheritance. He found him in a desert land, a howling wilderness; He encircled him, He instructed him, He kept him as the apple of His eye. . . . So the LORD alone led him."[2] And so the Lord will lead you, Moses implied.

What did David say to Saul when the king laughed at the shepherd boy who thought he could kill a giant? "The LORD, who delivered me from the paw of the lion and from the paw of the bear, He will deliver me from the hand of this Philistine."[3] David remembered God's help in the past and used that confirmation to give him courage for the future. Remembering how God has helped you in the past is a key to knowing that he will help you, too, in the present and in the future.

You see, David, the shepherd boy who became king, was really no different from you or me. He wasn't always a winner. In his early years, David, the author of the Twenty-third Psalm, also knew what it was to be rejected.

David's Many Rejections

First, David was rejected by his own father. When the prophet Samuel came to Jesse's home to seek the new king of Israel, Jesse gathered his sons to meet the prophet—six of them, but not the seventh and youngest, David.

Put yourself in David's shoes. Your dad calls all his sons together to tell them some wonderful news: "The prophet Samuel has come to anoint one of you as the future king of Israel. Get ready to meet him. . . . But not you, David. Someone must watch the sheep. You stay in the fields."

Second, David's own brother rejected him. When David brought supplies of dried grain and bread to his brothers who were with Saul's army, his oldest brother chastised him. "Why did you come? Why have you left the sheep?" David was repeatedly rejected as the little brother, the unwanted tagalong.

Third, David was rejected over and over again by King Saul. One moment David would be playing on his harp and singing a psalm to soothe Saul; the next moment he would be dodging a spear Saul had hurled at him. Saul made David earn Michal, Saul's daughter, for his wife by killing one hundred Philistines. Then, a few years later, he gave David's wife to another man, Paltiel. Rejection, not laud and honor and glory, was David's lot for many long, dark years.

Have you, too, felt rejected by a spouse or a parent or perhaps an employer? Have you ever been passed up for a promotion? Rejection strikes at the heart of each of us.

I was always the last one chosen for sports teams because I was built like a pear and was therefore an ungainly athlete. To this day I vividly remember the captains' choosing their players one by one until I was the last one left. Time and time again I suffered this rejection until I finally decided to do something about it. I started lifting weights at the end of my sophomore year, and by the end of my junior year my body had completely changed. I still weighed the same, but my flabby waist had moved up to my shoulders and turned into muscle. I joined the wrestling team that year and by my senior year, I had broken a couple of weight-lifting records. When I graduated from high school I was one of the strongest guys in school.

Rejection can cause our self-esteem, our self-dignity, to be destroyed. It's how we deal with rejection that makes the difference in our lives. I dealt positively with my rejection, and you can deal positively with yours.

David sat on the hills of Bethlehem, feeling totally rejected, while Samuel met with his father and brothers. The son whom Jesse expected to be chosen, Eliab, came before Samuel, and even the prophet thought, *Surely this is the Lord's annointed.*

But God stopped Samuel. He said, "Do not look at his appearance or at the height of his stature, because I have refused him. For the LORD does not see as man sees; for man looks at the outward appearance, but the LORD looks at the heart."[4]

When you are rejected by men, see yourself as God sees you. God sees where you are going, not where you've been. God sees what you're going to do, not what you've done.

Six sons passed before Samuel and the prophet said, "The Lord has not chosen these. Are all the young men here?"

"There remains yet the youngest, and there he is, keeping the sheep," Jesse replied.

"Send for him," Samuel ordered.

When David appeared before Samuel, the prophet said, "This is the one!"

David had the ruddy complexion and the bright eyes of youth. But David was chosen. The last was first, and the first was the last. When you're at the bottom, look up. Pray the prayer, "Shepherd me, Lord."

Where Am I Going?

Once you've taken a look at where you are, look toward the future. Too often we are tempted to agonize over our past mistakes and failures. The question is not, "Where have I come from?" but "Where am I going?" Unfortunately we are sometimes so upset by the tragedies we face that we feel as if we cannot function. We don't want to get up in the morning, we don't want to go to work, we don't want to see the people we have known for years. We simply want to stay in bed and pull the covers over our heads. We sit and mope and ask ourselves over and over again, "How could this have happened to me?" After all, the first verse of the Twenty-third Psalm says: "The Lord is my Shepherd. I shall not want."

Try asking yourself another question: what does this verse really mean? Friends of mine once admitted to me, "We have difficulty with that verse. It's one of the things that keep us from accepting the gospel. We know there are certain things we want that we don't have, yet the verse says, 'I shall not want.'"

I understood their confusion. If you study the Old Testament in its original language of Hebrew, you will see that this phrase translates: "I have no need." David is really saying, "I have no desire because God fills my every longing, my every hope, my every dream."

How does God fill your need? Write down the ways he has helped you in the past. After that, write down the positives in your life. My dad always told us to "turn your scars into stars." We all have things to be thankful for. Write them down. My own list during my going-through stage included a loving and supporting family—my mother and father and sisters—two children who loved me, friends who understood and cared about me, excellent physical health, and most important, an unswayingly positive faith in the God who loves me no matter what.

If you get lost in self-pity, if you continually shout at

God "Why me?" you can't get through the valley. You're stalled by bitterness and you can't begin to heal. There's a familiar saying: "God can't steer a parked car." You must make a definite decision to move ahead.

I took one step in this process the night before I told my congregation about my divorce. I sat on the balcony of the apartment a friend had lent me in Laguna Beach and looked up at the stars blinking and sparkling through the darkness.

"Oh, Lord," I prayed, "send your love to me as the stars above send their light through the billions of miles of hollow space. I feel as if eons have passed between me and the warmth of your tender touch.

"Please, Lord, shepherd me in grace, mercy, and peace. Shepherd me, Lord."

You, too, can pray such a prayer.

Look at your life positively. Then make a definite decision to move ahead, knowing God will help you get through your going-through stage. When God says, "Go!" I've learned to put on my track shoes and sprint ahead. Victory often lies in the future.

Finding Stars in Your Scars

One way to find the stars in your scars is to list the blessings you have, even though you may be going through some hard times. Take a moment now and list your blessings:

Relationships (Family or Friends):

1.

2.

3.

Spiritual Strengths:

1.

2.

3.

Career Opportunities:

1.

2.

3.

Health Blessings:

1.

2.

3.

Past Accomplishments:

1.

2.

3.

"[God] who has begun a good work in you will complete it."

When God says, "Go!"
put on
your track shoes.

STEP TWO

✣ ✣ ✣

When You're Down, Look Up!

"He makes me to lie down in green pastures."

I enjoy the tale of a conversation between former Prime Minister Menachem Begin of Israel and President Ronald Reagan during one of Begin's visits to America. Begin questioned the president about his platinum, red, and gold phones in the Oval Office. "Tell me, what are they really for?" he kidded the president.

"Well, the platinum phone goes to Republican headquarters so I can keep track of political affairs. The red phone is a hot line to Russia so I can keep track of what's happening there. My gold phone is a direct line to God."

"How much does it cost to call God?" Begin asked.

"Ten thousand dollars, but it's worth every penny."

Later when the president was visiting Prime Minister Begin in Israel, he asked the same question of Begin. "What are your three phones for?"

Begin replied, "One's a hot line to Egypt, another's a hot line to Parliament, and the third is a hot line to God."

"How much does it cost to call God from here?" Reagan asked the prime minister.

"Ten cents," Begin replied. "It's a local call."

The good news for those of us getting through the going-through stage is that we have a hot line to God. And guess what? It doesn't even cost a dime. It's free. By now you know that I'm talking about prayer. Nothing is more important at a time like this than praying a prayer of petition. "Comfort me, Lord." The second step you must take to get through the going-through stage is: when you're down, look up to the Good Shepherd.

The Book of Ecclesiastes says there's a time for all things. "A time to be born, a time to die." Now is the time for the prayer of petition. Sometimes when I suggest this to people who are hurting, they reply, "I didn't think I was allowed to pray for myself. I thought I was only supposed to pray for others."

Remember the first verse of the Twenty-third Psalm: "I shall not want." Or I shall have no need. God wants to fulfill your needs. The Greek word for prayer is *euchomai*, which has the connotation of "to wish, to want, to ask," and even in extreme cases, "to beg," as well as to pray. God expects us to ask him for our wants and our needs. Jesus told the parable of the persistent woman and the judge so that we would know we "always ought to pray and not lose heart."[1] This widow came to the judge to ask him to avenge a wrong that had been committed against her—not for a friend or a neighbor. She *was pleading for herself.*

Persistence Puts Power in Prayer

Whenever I feel my situation is hopeless, I think of this woman and her futile situation. First, she was a woman in biblical times, a position of obvious inferiority. (Read some of the rules in Deuteronomy if you don't believe me.) According to Jewish law, a wife was not allowed to divorce her husband for any reason, but a man could divorce his wife if he found any uncleanness in her.[2]

Second, she was a widow. This woman didn't have a husband to stand up for her or a male relative to represent her. She was completely on her own, probably penniless, with neither authority nor power.

Finally, the woman took her petition, "Avenge me of my adversary," to a judge who admitted he had no moral standards or human compassion. "I do not fear God nor regard man,"[3] he said.

The first time this woman came to the judge she was turned away. But she returned again and again. Each time she was denied justice. Nevertheless, she persisted. She continued to return each day. Finally, the judge decided, *The only way I'll ever get rid of this woman is to give her her day in court.*

This woman came to an unjust judge. We come to a righteous Father. This woman had no one to speak for her. We have an advocate before the Father, his own Son, Jesus Christ, our intercessor. This woman was not invited to speak to the judge. We are allowed to ask and we are promised that our needs will be met.

E. Stanley Jones, the well-known missionary to India, often conducted renewal meetings for spiritual growth, which he called ashrams. He began each ashram by saying, "Pull out a piece of paper and a pen or pencil and write down your want or your need today."

I suggest that you do the same thing this moment. Write your need in your day book or journal or on the page provided at the end of this chapter. If you say, "I don't have a need," repeat E. Stanley Jones's answer to those who made such a reply to him: "If you think you don't have a need, that is your need."

Now write a short prayer for your need and say the prayer throughout the day, morning, afternoon, and evening, persistently like the widow. Jesus challenges you. If even an evil judge will listen, God, your heavenly Father, will surely give justice to his people who plead with him day and night.

I'll never forget the day I read through the long lists of begats in First Chronicles. It was not the first time I had read the list, but instead of being lulled to sleep by the repetition of "Abraham begat Isaac" and "Isaac begat Jacob," I suddenly relaized that in the fourth chapter the rhythm stopped with the mention of Jabez who asked God to bless him. *And he did.*[4] What a perfect example of the answer to prayer. Only one man in all the long lists asked God to bless him. And of course, he did.

And he will bless us, too.

Again and again I prayed during those difficult days following my divorce. "Comfort me, Lord." Did God reply to my prayer? Will he reply to yours?

When I announced our impending divorce to the congregation on that Sunday in January of 1984, I felt as if I was attending my own funeral. I thought my ministry was over. I had no idea what to expect from the congregation. I sat in the pulpit chair with my head down. Within seconds I heard the sound of footsteps crossing the wooden floor, then coming up the steps and onto the platform. I looked up and everyone was gathering around me. Members of the congregation hugged me and said, "We love you. We will do all we can to help. We are going to see you through this trial."

To me, God was saying, "Your ministry is not over. It may just be beginning." The phrase, "Every end is a new beginning," kept coming into my mind throughout that day.

The next Sunday I told the congregation, "I want to thank you for the support you've been giving me. That support reminds me of the miraculous growth of the majestic redwood trees of California. Most trees have root structures that are just as wide and just as deep as their leaf lines are wide and high. The redwood is the one exception. Its low-lying roots spread across the ground in many different directions, instead of reaching deep into the earth. As the redwood grows higher and higher, its root structure only grows wider, not deeper. Theoretically, a redwood cannot stand alone!

"But then, redwoods always grow *together*. Two, three, four, until they form a forest, and their root structures intertwine with each other. Redwoods hold each other up. Together they are strong, and together they become the tallest trees in the world. I have not been alone, because I am a part of this church. You have allowed me to keep growing, even though my marriage has failed. Thank you."

The Comfort of His People

How does God comfort his people? Through other people. I like to sing the words of this song: "I am the Church. You are the Church. We are the Church together. All who follow Jesus all around the world. We are the church together."

Songwriter Roger Williams says that his father always said:

There is so much good in the worst of us
And so much bad in the best of us
It hardly becomes any of us to talk about the rest of us.

Sometimes we're so busy criticizing others for sins they've committed, we forget that the church is here to comfort and to care. We are not here to condemn. We are here to open our arms as wide as Christ does and to say, "Wherever you are in your life—down and out or depressed or addicted to drugs or alcohol—we love you. We care about you."

After the Second World War, the townspeople of one devastated city in England were concerned about the restoration of a large statue of Jesus that had been symbolic of Christ's help and guidance for many generations. It had stood in the city square with hands outstretched in an attitude of invitation. The words carved on the pedestal read: "Come to me."

Master artists and sculptors worked for months reassembling the figure. But not enough fragments from the hands could be found in the rubble to mend them. Finally someone suggested, "The sculptors can make new hands."

The townspeople rejected the proposal. "Leave him without hands!" they decided.

Today the restored statue of Christ stands in the square without hands. The words carved on the new pedestal read: "Christ has no hands but ours."

Someone wrote this short poem after seeing the statue:

I have no hands but your hands to do my work today.
I have no feet but your feet to lead men on the way.
I have no tongue but your tongue to tell men how I died.
I have no help but your help to bring men to God's side.

This is not too different from the commission Christ gave to his disciples before the left the earth. "Go therefore and make disciples of all the nations, baptizing them in the name of the Father and of the Son and of the Holy Spirit."[5]

Christ expects us to help other people. But we cannot help others and they cannot help us if we will not share our problems. We must be willing to take some risks.

Several weeks before I told the congregation about my divorce, I had gone to see Dr. Herman Ridder, associate pastor of the Crystal Cathedral.

"A pastor traditionally deals with divorce in one of two ways," he said, "The first is never to mention his divorce or marital problems to anyone. He just ignores them. If somebody mentions his impending divorce, he simply replies, 'That's my personal life. I'd rather not discuss it.' In most cases, this is not the best way.

"Another approach is to give the congregation an opportunity to support you and minister to you. I suggest that approach."

I chose to risk it. I opened my life to the congregation, and the people responded by reaching out in love.

The Comfort of His Presence

Another way God comforts us is by reaching out to us himself. I realized this one day when I visited a teenage boy who suffered from leukemia in a Los Angeles hospital. His bone marrow had been destroyed, and he didn't have any white blood cells to fight off simple diseases like the common cold. For weeks he sat in a little plastic room, ten feet square, in Children's Hospital in Los Angeles.

To reach his room, I walked down a one-hundred-foot corridor of plastic tarps crackling as they moved back and forth. I wasn't allowed to enter his plastic room, which he had decorated with posters of rock singers, his stereo, his books, and a table and chair. Instead, I stood in the doorway, dressed in a hospital gown, talking to him through the plastic.

I noticed a tiny baby girl lying in a little hospital bed in the room next to him. Her parents hadn't touched or held this baby for months.

"How can the baby feel love?" I asked the nurse.

"Oh, we can still love her," she replied. The young woman put her hands into plastic arms that had been fashioned into the tarp; the plastic wall bent in toward the crib. She picked up the baby, cradling her securely in one arm so she could lower the sides of the bed, and then sat down on it so she could hold the baby on her lap. She kissed the plastic and the plastic pressed against the cheek of this little baby who'd just celebrated her first birthday inside this bubble. She bounced the baby on her lap; she rocked the baby back and forth. The baby's musical coos and laughter made it obvious she felt the nurse's love.

Then the nurse went to the next plastic room to see a little boy who looked about five years old. "Hi, Josh," she said. "How are you?"

"Oh, I'm doing pretty good," he answered from inside the bubble. The nurse stuck her hands into another set of plastic arms and began boxing with the little boy. In a few weeks the plastic walls between Joshua and the nurse and his parents were going to be torn down. Soon they would be able to touch cheek-to-cheek.

Those plastic walls are similar to the division between God and ourselves. We can't see God. We can't touch him. But we can feel his presence, just as that baby and Joshua felt the nurse's love. God comforts us during the going-through stage if we confess our problems and just ask him, "Comfort me, Lord."

Unfortunately, some of us are so bitter about the struggles we face, we turn from God rather than toward him. Still others won't admit that they have any flaws, even to God. They think they can get along without God. But time reveals their error.

People are similar to many of the marble statues of ancient times. These statues appeared to be flawlessly carved from solid marble. But many were really flawed. Every once in a while the sculptor slipped and cut too deeply because the tools ancient sculptors used were crude.

To remedy this, the sculptors filled in the chips with wax and sold the statues anyway. After a few months in the heat, the wax began to melt. Cracks and pitholes began to appear. An arm might fall off. Customers learned to look on the bottom of the statue for the Latin word *sincera*, which meant "without wax." The word assured the consumer that the statue was a sincere work of perfection. It was all real. One hundred percent marble or granite. Sincere.

We need to be honest with our maker. We need to say, "Here I am. I've got a scar over here. This is me, Lord. Imperfect. Damaged. I don't have the capability to break through the barrier of sin and reach heaven on my own. But I'm *sincere*! My love for you is real!"

Once we've admitted our faults to ourselves and the Lord, he can pick us up. He can mold and shape us into perfect creatures and present us to God, his Father, pure and clean and spotless.

I like the translation of the second verse of the Twenty-third Psalm in the Living Bible: "He lets me rest in the meadow grass." Every time I read this verse I think of the beautiful hills of Galilee. In the winter they are bathed by refreshing rains and become as green as the lush growth of the Hawaiian Islands. As the weather warms, the green blades of the daffodil begin to spin in the wind. Then the daffodils and other flowers appear. Splashes of yellows, fiery reds, the bright oranges dot the rolling meadows. When summer comes with its heat and wind, the hills turn to a soft, lulling brown until the miracle of regeneration begins again as it has for centuries.

David, the writer of the Twenty-third Psalm, knew those hills well. As a shepherd boy he had grazed his sheep there, sleeping by his herd or relaxing on a soft, matted bed of grass as he ate or played his harp. Later, when he was pursued by Saul and his life was in danger, David compared God's love and care in the midst of such violence to the peace he felt in those Galilean hills.

When I read his words, I realize that the same loving, dependable God cares for me and wishes to give me that same comfort and peace.

My Lord *lets* me lie down in the meadow grass. He isn't forcing me to do things that are against my desires or my needs. He's granting me a rest from my problems. When you've put in a full day and you're weary and you've had an argument with the boss, remember this verse and pray the words of petition: "Comfort me, Lord." When you're waiting to get the results of a biopsy, pray the prayer, "Comfort me, Lord."

The Comfort of His Word

How does God comfort us? First, through his people, the church. Second, by reaching out to us himself. And finally, through the messages of our own ministers and other preachers.

Sometimes hurting people tell me, "I can't come to church. I cry every time I go to a service."

I always answer, "Do you know what you're missing? You're missing God's grace for you, his comfort."

It's a shame that people who hurt are afraid to cry in church. Where else should we be free to cry if not among God's people?

Other people are so bitter about the struggles they face, they refuse to attend church or have anything to do with religion. If you doubt that God can reach you through a minister's message, let me share with you the story of Shannon Wilkerson, a young woman who was helped by the "Hour of Power," my father's Sunday television program.

Shannon's mother was an alcoholic. "Many times as a child," Shannon says, "I can remember crawling underneath my dresser and being very quiet so my mother couldn't find me. As I grew up, I was afraid of being friendly with the other kids. I didn't want them to come home with me and see my mom. In high school I began experimenting with drugs, which helped me to fit in.

"Often I would go to sleep at night with the TV on because I was so afraid of being alone. One morning I woke up and there was this minister saying, 'Don't turn that channel because Jesus has something for you today.'

"I didn't know that much about Jesus. But that morning, Dr. Schuller's message really touched my heart. He made me believe that I could be great. I could be different from my mother.

"Sunday after Sunday I kept tuning back to 'The Hour of Power,' and Dr. Schuller kept giving me the encouragement and strength I needed to stay away from drugs. Then I started testing the Lord. I began with little things. I wanted to play first-chair clarinet in the high school orchestra. So I prayed and I practiced the positive thinking Dr. Schuller talked about and it happened. I wanted to raise champion animals in the Future Farmers of America, and that happened, too.

"Then I was ready to ask for the greatest miracle of all: for my mother to stay sober. I prayed about it. I read Dr. Schuller's books. I wrote 'The Hour of Power,' and I was told that alcoholism was a disease. 'You're not responsible for your mother's alcoholism,' they told me, which really helped since I had always felt I had done something to make my mother become an alcoholic.

"I hadn't, but I was a co-alcoholic, someone who feeds the disease by his or her reactions. I would often search for my mother's hidden bottles and then flash them in her face and say, 'You're an alcoholic!' One time I called Alcoholics Anonymous and asked them to take her to an AA metting. When they came, my mother screamed, 'I'm not an alcoholic! Get these people out of my house!'

"I prayed and prayed. Yet nothing seemed to happen. Finally I decided to take her last bottle after she had passed out one afternoon. I knew that you weren't supposed to do that to an alcoholic, but I did it anyway. That evening, when I was talking to a friend on the phone, my mother came up behind me and screamed, 'Shannon, I hate you! I want to kill you!'

"I thought, *Well, here goes. Another fight.* But when I turned around I saw a knife in her hand. I slammed down the phone and ran to my bedroom. Mom stumbled a few times so I was able to lock the door before she reached my room.

"She stood outside screaming, 'Shannon, I hate you! I wish you were dead! I hate you!' Then I heard a thud and the knife came through the door. I looked at the tip of that knife, and I felt all my hope shatter. I fell into a clump on the floor and cried. I was angry at God. *Why would you let this happen?* I screamed at him. *I've prayed. I've had faith.*

"I listened for an answer. In that moment of quietness, I heard God speak to me. He said, 'Shannon, get up off your knees, open that door, and tell your mother that you are sorry.'

"I thought, *You've got to be kidding. That woman just tried to kill me. There's no way I'm going to tell her I'm sorry.* But I felt the peace of the Holy Spirit come upon me. It was as if he picked me up and made me open the door. Lying there on the floor in front of me was a very sick, ugly woman. Suddenly, I felt sorry for her rather than me. The words naturally came to my lips. 'Mom, I'm sorry that it's like this. I love you very much. And I'm sorry.'

"It was as if an incredible burden had been lifted from my shoulders. You see, I wasn't really telling my mother I was sorry. I was telling Shannon. 'I'm sorry that you have allowed your mother's problem to become your problem. I'm sorry that this problem has taken control of your life. Now, you go out there and be great.'

"And that's what I did. The fights kept occurring. But every time I said, 'I'm sorry, Mom. I'm sorry it's like this.' One day when I came home from school I felt a peace in the house. I went into my bedroom as I always did, and my mother came in. She put her arms around me and said, 'Shannon, I'm very, very sick. I have a disease. It's called alcoholism. I've called AA, and they're coming to pick me up. I'm scared, Shannon. I just want you to know that I love you very, very much.'

"It was the first time in my life my mother had really told me she loved me. And I believed her. I knew it would work this time. She went to AA that night and for many weeks afterward.... That miracle came true. Today my mother and her new husband, who is also a recovered alcoholic, travel all over the country sharing their stories with other alcoholics. My mother's been sober for more than eleven years.

"It hurts me to listen to her tell people how much she hated me. It hurts me to hear her say that I represented everything she wasn't. I was young. My life was ahead of me. She felt hers was over. But she always ends by saying, 'My daughter is twenty-eight years old today and I am eleven.' I thank God for giving me my mother."

Impossibilities do become possibilities. Prayer is answered. Persistence does pay off. God does speak to us today. He is active in the affairs of you and me. All we have to do is pray for his comfort and expect to receive it.

Sharing Our Needs with God

One of the best ways to share your needs with God is to write them out on paper and then to write a prayer you can repeat throughout the day to petition God with these needs. Use this page to list your needs and to write your prayer of petition.

My greatest needs right now are:

1.

2.

3.

My prayer of petition is:

O, Lord,______________________________________

____

____

____Amen.

Risks

To laugh is to risk appearing the fool.
To weep is to risk appearing sentimental.
To reach out to another is to risk involvement.
To expose feelings is to risk exposing your true self.
To place your ideas and dreams before a crowd is to risk
their loss.
To love is to risk not being loved in return.
To live is to risk dying.
To hope is to risk despair.
To try is to risk failure.

But risks must be taken because the greatest hazard in
life is to risk nothing.
The person who risks nothing does nothing,
has nothing and is nothing.
He may avoid suffering and sorrow, but he cannot learn,
feel, change, grow, or live.
Chained by his certitudes, he is a slave; he has
forfeited his freedom.
Only a person who risks is free.

—author unknown

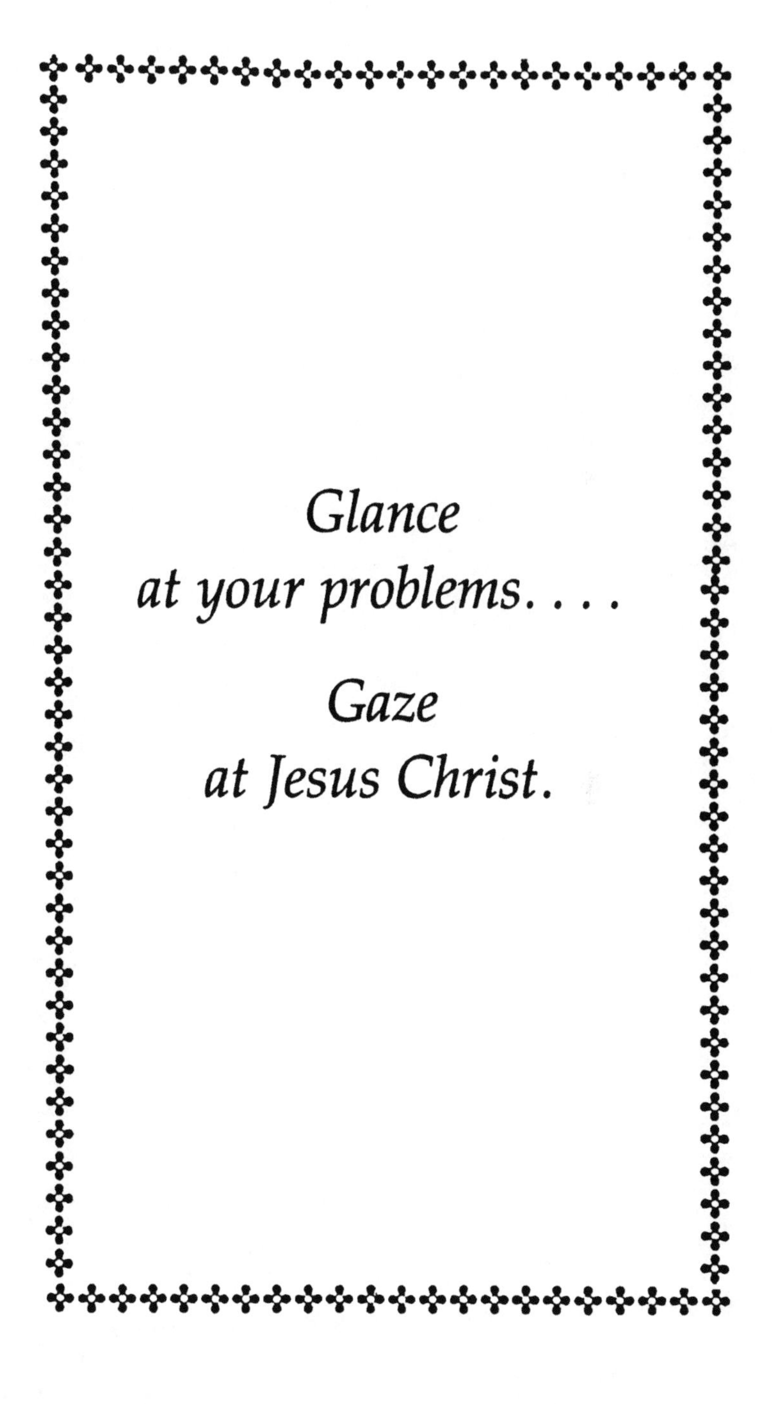

Glance
at your problems. . . .

Gaze
at Jesus Christ.

STEP THREE

✣ ✣ ✣

Think of God as Your Partner.

"He leads me beside the still waters. He restores my soul."

Whether we are aware of it or not, we are all following some guide—some philosophy—for our lives. Some of us stumble along and really don't realize we are following a guide. Others make a definite decision to follow a philosophy like materialism, humanism, Buddhism, or Christianity.

I was reminded of how important a guide is to us when I visited my sister Carol in Winter Park, Colorado, in the winter of 1984. Carol had been living there for three years, learning to ski with only one leg. When she was thirteen years old, her leg had to be amputated after it was crushed in a serious motorcycle accident. This young girl, who had faced such tragedy only six years earlier, was now acting as my guide and ski instructor in Colorado.

Carol took control almost immediately. "Bob, you can't ski with those clothes!" she said when I opened my suitcase at the motel. "You've got to get a warmer outfit."

I looked at the pair of Levi's, a sweater, and a medium-weight jacket, my normal southern California attire. They seemed okay to me, but I respected her expertise. I didn't object when she suggested we visit a sporting goods store to buy the proper equipment. Since she was my guide, I followed her advice.

First, she suggested that I buy ski pants, which zipped up the sides so I could take them off without removing my skis and boots. Then she suggested that I buy a down parka, some thermal underwear, and a pair of thermal leather gloves. The bill was much more costly than I had planned, but later that day, when I was sitting on the chair lift, shivering as it inched its way to the top of the beginners' slope, I was glad that I had purchased the special clothing.

It had never occurred to me that I could get lost in Winter Park. I'd only skied a couple of times when I was ten years old on the bunny runs at a resort in Big Bear Lake, California, which at that time consisted of two rope tows that pulled skiers to the top of a run of only one hundred yards. But at Winter Park I sat on a chair lift for thirty minutes to climb to the top of the main mountain, an elevation of fourteen thousand feet.

Once I reached the top, I looked down to see a bottom that was so far below me it was shrouded by clouds. I was glad I had a guide. In fact, I got nervous every time Carol was more than one hundred yards ahead of me. The skiing was great that weekend because my sister, who was an alternate for the handicapped Olympic team that year and who knew Winter Park, served as my personal guide.

But what if I'd had a poor guide? I know I could have chosen a ski run that was far too advanced and broken my arm or leg since I hadn't skied in twenty years. Carol spent a lot of time shouting instructions at me. "Don't bend over! Stand up straight! Use your legs!" I benefited greatly from such a conscientious guide. In fact, the guide I choose makes a great difference in any trip I take.

I've supervised more than fifteen hundred people on twelve different trips to the Holy Land, and I know how an informed guide can make a site come alive. I remember one guide who took me to Capernaum. He led us to the entrance to the temple. Then he stopped and asked me, "Robert, how many times have you been to Israel?"

"I don't know," I replied. "Probably fifteen or sixteen times."

"And how many times have you been to Capernaum?"

"Every time I come, I always come to Capernaum."

"Then you know what these two holes were used for." He pointed to two holes in the stoop that surrounded the steps to the temple.

I looked at the dishlike holes in the top of this giant stone and realized that I'd never even noticed them before. "I have no idea," I admitted.

"That's because I'm one of the few guides who know what these holes are. I have participated in some of the digs and studied with the archaeologists. These two holes were the dishes used by the temple money changers. As you know, Caesar's money was not used in the temple. So visitors put the Roman money in one dish and the money changer gave them the equivalent Hebrew money from the other dish."

The guide you choose makes all the difference on a trip, as you can see; the guide you choose in life is just as important. Let's review briefly the various philosophies one might choose today.

Materialism

Today people have many guides to choose from and many paths to follow. Some select materialism, a philosophy expressed by the bumper sticker: "The one who ends up with the most toys wins." Materialistic people think, "Am I going to get more points if I do this or that?" They never wonder, "Am I going to hurt people? What am I really getting from a larger house or a bigger boat?"

Most of us sympathize with the thousands of Ohioans who in 1985 invested their savings in one of that state's sixty-nine chartered savings and loan associations, only to have the S & Ls closed by the state government because they were near financial collapse. Those who invested in New York City bonds also lost their money in 1972. There is no monetary security in this world. True security must come from some other source. While financial stability is important, remember, "Nobody takes a U-Haul to heaven."

Humanism

Another choice might be humanism, which seems to be the prevalent guide today. "If it's not going to hurt anybody, it's okay."

As an ancient philosophy, humanism focused upon man's free will and the creation of ideals and values for him to abide by. This way of life was examined and endorsed by a wide variety of thinkers, including the author Boccaccio, the statesman Machiavelli, and even such churchmen as Thomas More and Erasmus.

Over the years, however, humanism has become so intently focused on man's free will, its followers today claim that they are the complete masters of their fate and that no God exists who can control them. There are factions among both the Protestant and Catholic churches that believe that although God may exist, he does not respond to prayer or inspire believers or interfere in any way with the lives of human beings. These people believe that God has abandoned them. They are alone.

Religion

Still another choice is to accept a religious philosophy as a guide. All religions of the world can generally be divided into two camps: the Eastern religions and the Judaic religions. Eastern religions are Buddhism, Hinduism, Confucianism, Taoism, and smaller sects such as the Hare Krishnas. The Judaic religions are Judaism, Islam, and Christianity.

E. Stanley Jones often tells the story of a discussion he had with a Buddhist monk. Stanley asked the monk, "Is there life after death?"

"Why, of course not," the monk answered.

"What is there, then?" Stanley asked.

"Nothingness."

Stanley says that the Buddhist philosophy grew out of the monks' search for the answer to the question. "How do we eliminate suffering and pain from this world?" After grappling with this question for generations, the monks decided that a state of nothingness, or Nirvana, was the only answer.

I don't know how you would define Nirvana, but to me, it is death. All of the Eastern religions point toward a state of nothingness as man's destiny. If that's the end you desire, an Eastern religion is for you.

The Judaic religions offer another option. They share a common belief in life after death. These religions have a common ancestor, Abraham, and a common history, which can be found in the Jewish Talmud and the first five books of the Old Testament.

Judaism offers life after death, but it is limited by a series of laws, the Torah, which must be performed before someone can be saved. In biblical times a Jew sacrificed an animal in the temple as a means of atonement if he disobeyed the laws. Now that the temple has been destroyed, atonement is not available to the Jew. So I ask the question, "According to the Jewish law and traditions, do Jews have a means of salvation?" I don't know of an answer to that question. I see no means of life after death in the Jewish faith.

Strict obedience to certain laws and traditions is also essential to salvation in the Islamic faith. The mechanic who works on my car is Islamic. One day when he was writing up the work order for my car, he found out that I was a minister. He put down his pencil and we discussed religion together for three hours.

During the conversation he explained the Islam belief with a simple drawing. First he drew a picture of a stick man. Then he drew a tightrope underneath the man and at the end of the rope a circle for heaven. "Life is a tightrope, and at the end of the rope is heaven," he explained.

Then underneath the rope he drew a large circle for hell. "If you are good, you will be able to walk the tightrope into heaven," he explained. "If you haven't been good, you won't be able to walk that tightrope. You will fall into hell." To me, hell is another form of death, more brutal than nothingness.

Christianity is the only religion that offers life and the *assurance* of salvation. The promise is: "Whoever believes in Him [Jesus Christ] should not perish but have everlasting life."[1] Life after death for those who believe in Jesus is not nothingness or hell but life without pain and sorrow with God, the Father.

Unfortunately, people sometimes deny God's existence. For instance, some intellectuals feel that religion is too simplistic. In 1984 Dr. Ellen Bening, a sociologist and editor for doctrinal dissertations at the School of Human Behavior at the United States International University in San Diego, wrote my dad. She had heard him speak at my church the Sunday before.

"My reason for coming that Sunday was that two weeks earlier I had listened for the first time to a televised service from the Crystal Cathedral," she admitted. "On other occasions I turned to other channels in search of nonreligious programs. However, your sermon on life's contradictions captured my attention. You spoke about the contradictions in areas such as physics and ethics and about the possibility of resolving contradictions through positive perception and action.

"You also demonstrated that it is not a contradiction to be a deeply reflective, reasoning human being and an adamantly faithful Christian. I had heard it said in Bible study classes that rationality should be set aside in matters of religion. 'Reasoning involves questioning, questioning can generate doubt, and doubt is opposed to faith,' some said.

"After hearing your sermon I could not stop thinking about its diverse applications. I thought, for example, about existential philosophy and the theater of the absurd, popular on campuses in the sixties, which focused on portraying the contradictions in life. Although I never enjoyed reading existential literature, in retrospect I see how effective it was in showing that in confronting contradictions, man can adopt a perspective which leads toward spiritual darkness. He can select a path to a dead end and despair.

"I also began to think about the alternative path which Christ offered, and for the first time I began not only to see but to feel the precious gift he gives. When I awakened on that Sunday, the 26th of August, I had the feeling that perhaps I was ready to receive that gift.

"My husband and I arrived early enough to be the

first seated in the first row. As the church began to fill with people, I thought back on the many times I had felt alienated in churches. That feeling had vanished. In its place was a sense of belonging and joy, the kind of feeling one had when returning home after a long, strenuous trip. I had decided to dress in white that day. The choice felt appropriate.

"Your sermon, entitled 'Breaking Through: There's Hope for You,' focused on faith. I had imagined that certain fortunate people experienced a calling from God, were mystically touched, felt a spiritual awakening, and hence received faith. It never occurred to me that faith is an option.

"I experienced a birth in the church that day, and I am amazed at how simple it really was! God only asked me to have enough faith to listen and to travel a few miles to a church. After spending twenty-two of my thirty-four years as a student in one or another school, I had assumed that I would have to pass some monumental test before I would be qualified to take my rightful place in a church. Faith seemed like another degree, the most advanced of degrees, one earned after unlocking the secrets of the universe.

"But in reality God asked so little and gave in return so much! He is there to guide in all I do. No longer must I live with the intolerable weight of believing that all my decisions and problems must be mine and mine alone. God gave a friend who can help in countless ways. Of course I select the option of faith! Having known the alternative, I know that no matter how difficult life may become, it can never be as dark as it was living without the knowledge that the Lord is my shepherd."

The decision this anthropologist made is open to all of us. If you haven't stopped to consider "Who or what is my guide in life?" now is the time to do it. Often we ask questions during the going-through stage that we don't ask when our lives seem to be going very well. Finally ask yourself, "Is there another guide that might be better?"

I certainly cannot prove the existence of God to you.

But I can look at the influence that God's word, the Bible, and a belief in him have on the hearts and minds and lives of people around me. As Immanuel Kant said, when one has to make a decision on a moral issue, he can ask the question, "If everybody in the world did this thing, would the world be a better place?"

The letters that come in daily to "The Hour of Power" give hundreds of examples of lives changed for the better. Let me tell you about two I read recently.

A young man from Rochester, New York, wrote: "When I was fourteen years old, I was diagnosed as having muscular dystrophy. Right away I began to feel bitter. I became a troublemaker at school. At age sixteen I was expelled, and I began drinking and fighting with my adoptive dad. Then I started doing drugs as an escape. Soon I began to depend on drugs.

"One day I turned on the television to the 'Hour of Power.' I couldn't believe the positive attitude I was hearing from Dr. Schuller and his daughter, Carol. I just wished that I could feel like them.

"Three-and-one-half years ago I asked God for forgiveness and let him know that for the first time I believed in him and wanted him to come into my life. My life has changed completely. I no longer smoke, do drugs, drink, or swear."

The second letter was sent to me from a woman in Carolina, Puerto Rico, who had heard one of my messages on 'The Hour of Power,' which is carried by the ARMS network of stations around the world. Her two-sentence letter read: "Please pray with me for the forgiveness of my sins. And to thank God for his many blessings." Inside the envelope with the letter was a makeshift money pouch made out of a magazine cover. A quarter was pasted inside. I almost cried when I saw it.

What happens to the lives of people when the existence of God becomes a reality in their hearts? They become better people. Through research, *Psychology Today* also came to this conclusion. In 1981 this magazine conducted a survey of its readers "to learn how people would resolve some typical moral dilemmas and what choices they would make in particular situations." The magazine received 24,100 completed questionnaires accompanied by about 4,000 letters, the largest number ever received in a *PT* survey. They tabulated the responses and then looked at how the choices people made were related to other characteristics such as age, sex, occupation, and religiousness.

Psychology Today concluded, "The most significant predictor of a person's moral behavior may be religious commitment. People who consider themselves very religious were least likely to report deceiving their friends, having extramarital affairs, cheating on their expense accounts, or even parking illegally."[2]

What happens to the lives of people when the existence of God becomes a reality in their hearts? They become better people. The third step in getting through the going-through stage is: choose God as your partner and guide.

A Partnership with God

The Twenty-third Psalm begins with the words, *The Lord is my shepherd.* The psalm then promises that if we choose God as our partner and guide, we shall not want. The key word here is *choose*. We are not sheep who automatically follow someone else. We must surrender our wills to the guide's; we must trust him with our lives, just as the blind skiers did when I was at Winter Park.

I didn't see these skiers at first. To notice them you have to be close enough to see the words *Blind Skier* on the bibs they wear over their coats or to hear their lead skiers, fifteen to thirty feet ahead of them, calling, "Left. Right. Slow down." The blind skiers cannot see their instructors or the slope or the trees or the pitfalls ahead of them. They must put their faith totally and completely in the instructors and their words.

That's the commitment God needs from us. That trust. That faith. That's why we pray the prayer, "Guide me, Lord," and pray it over and over again, day after day, month after month, year after year. I'm sure those blind skiers must be afraid each time they face a more difficult slope or learn a new technique of skiing. Each day they must renew their faith in their instructors, just as we must again surrender our wills to the Shepherd's.

As a minister I had already made a choice to follow God as my guide, but during my going-through stage I had to ask myself, "Have I given God control of my life?" This is a difficult step for most of us. We want to think that we're in complete control of our lives. But are we really? Let me tell you the story of Gene, a thirty-eight-year-old salesman.

After a couple of years of marriage, Gene's wife wanted a divorce. They went to a counselor together, but Gene's wife, June, could not see any hope of reconciliation. "I just don't feel anything for him anymore," she said. Finally she admitted, "I have a new boyfriend who is really exciting!"

Gene was totally perplexed. He was extremely good-looking and had always been popular. In the next months he went through a period of self-searching, trying to understand what he had done wrong. He mentioned real and imagined foibles to his counselor, any reason he could think of that would cause June to leave him.

Most of the time his counselor had to say, "Well, Gene, that may be true about you. Maybe you are that way, but you're only human. Let's not use that as an explanation of why June left you."

Gene was trying to hold on to the myth that he had complete control over his life. His counselor says, "I think many people want to feel as if they have control over their lives. If they can identify mistakes they've made, then they're in control and can correct those mistakes in the future."

Instead Gene had to admit that he was a victim, which was both a disappointment and a relief to him. Gene had to admit he was not in control of what had happened to him. Then he had to renew his decision to allow God to control his life.

What happens when we allow God to control our lives? Miraculous occurrences. Accomplishments we could never achieve on our own.

I will never forget a story told to me by Corrie ten Boom, the Dutch woman who spent months in prison and in the Ravensbrueck concentration camp for hiding Jews during the Second World War. I was sitting in her living room with some other guests after enjoying a Sunday brunch at her home. Corrie was talking about the strain that those awful days in prison had put on her own faith. She turned to her assistant and asked her to go outside and get a few blades of grass and put them in a jar. Then she held up the jar so everyone in the room could see it.

"You see these blades of grass," she said. "They remind me of the days I was in solitary confinement. I prayed, 'God, how much longer do I have to take this? If you're alive, if you really care, will you please show me a sign that you are alive and that you hear my prayers?' "

That night Corrie lay down on her cot feeling totally abandoned and alone. She fell asleep crying and wondering why God wouldn't answer her prayers. The next morning, when Corrie woke up, a beam of light was shining down through a crack in the ceiling on a few blades of green grass. A miracle in the middle of that concrete cell!

"I knew without any doubt," Corrie told us, "that God was alive and that his light would shine again in my life in a beautiful and wonderful way, even though the possibility seemed impossible."

That morning Corrie's faith in God and her commitment to allow him to control her life were renewed. And the impossibility of living through her imprisonment became a possibility in the next months through some mysterious quirk of what some people call "fate."

At first this "fate" seemed to be certain death, for Corrie was transferred to the dreaded Ravensbrueck camp. Here she joined her sister, Betsie, until she died in the camp at the end of 1944. Betsie's last words to Corrie were, ". . . must tell the people what we have learned here. We must tell them that there is no pit so deep that He is not deeper still. They will listen to us, Corrie, because we have been here."

Corrie could not believe what Betsie was saying. "But when will all this happen, Betsie!" she asked.

"Now. Right away. Oh, very soon! By the first of the year, Corrie, we will be out of prison!"[3]

Betsie died the next day. And two days later Corrie's name was called over the loudspeaker. She was taken into the administration barracks and led into a room where several prisoners stood in front of a large desk. To her amazement, the officer behind the desk said, "*Eltassen!*" to the prisoner directly in front of him. Released!

For no reason that Corrie knew, she was given a certificate of discharge that day and then sent to the prison hospital until the edema in her badly swollen legs healed. Corrie ten Boom walked out of Ravensbrueck on New Year's Day of 1945. Both she and her sister, Betsie, were free!

In the spring of 1945 Corrie began describing those days in Ravensbrueck to her countrymen in Holland. She lived for thirty-eight more years, telling millions of people throughout the world about the God who sustained her through one of the darkest moments of human history.

When we allow God to control our lives, miraculous occurrences are possible because of the power of the Holy Spirit.

Now Tap into the Power

Once we allow God to control our lives, we need to open ourselves to the inspiration of the Holy Spirit. The word *inspire* actually means "to breathe the breath of life into."

Think of the times you've huffed and puffed and puffed and huffed to blow up a balloon. Then all at once the flat, rubbery blob responds and becomes a large, colorful balloon that can float high, high into the sky. That's just how the inspiration of the Holy Spirit can transform our lives.

Nate Morrison, that stalwart member of my church, often tells how the Holy Spirit inspired him to help me found the Rancho Capistrano Community Church.

Nate had looked for a church in southern Orange County for quite some time. Every once in a while he drove to Garden Grove to attend the Crystal Cathedral, but more often he watched "The Hour of Power" on television. "I was an electronic Christian," Nate admits.

Nate was listening to "The Hour of Power" the Sunday I told about my dream to start my own church in San Juan Capistrano. His first reaction was, *Oh, that's nice. Maybe I ought to visit that church once it gets started.* The next moment he heard a voice say, "You are going to help this young man get this church going." The voice was real enough to Nate that the hair on his arms and on the back of his neck stood up.

The words *Who me?* quickly came into his mind. After all, he hadn't been a member of an organized church for quite a few years. But when you're inspired by the Holy Spirit, all objections seem to be inconsequential.

The next week Nate contacted me and offered his services to the church. As you know from reading the earlier chapters of this book, he was an active force in the fledgling years of this church and now has become a full-time assistant, conducting Bible studies, making hospital visits, and counseling our members.

Some people experience God's guidance as Nate did. Others find guidance through his word in the Bible. I believe that three actions allow us to utilize the Holy Spirit's power, *listen*, *learn*, and *lift*. Let's begin with listen.

Listen

In the Book of Revelation, Christ warns the church of Ephesus, "He who has an ear, let him hear."[4] Be careful to listen to all the positives coming to you today, for God seldom speaks in negatives. The negatives kill. They destroy. I didn't realize how much power negative words and emotions have until I went with a friend to visit his relative in the hospital when I was sixteen years old. The man lay in the bed, gasping for air; tubes were attached to his arm and other parts of his body, and his color was so pale his face blended with the sheets. He could grunt a little and squirm a little, but that was all.

My friend and I stood next to his bed. "Do you think he's going to make it?" I asked after a while.

"It doesn't look like it, does it?" my friend answered. During the next minutes my friend and I continued to discuss the man's condition.

About three weeks later, my father asked if I'd like to make a hospital visit with him. Before we entered the room, Dad said, "Robert, the man you are about to see is not well. He may only grunt or squeeze our hands. But whatever you do, do not say a negative word.

"Hold his hand. Tell him he's going to live. Tell him God is with him; he will guide and take care of him. Consciously or subconsciously, he'll hear your words."

Dad held the man's hand and said just that. Then he asked the man to listen while he prayed for him. I also spoke encouragingly to the man.

That man seemed closer to death than my friend's relative. But he lived and the other man died. I have no idea whether or not our words influenced what happened, but I feel as if I might have added to the one man's distress and lightened the other's. I know now that the Holy Spirit uses me and he uses you to speak positively to other people.

We choose what we listen to. We choose the thoughts we think. We choose the way we see situations. We can say, "It's finished. I'm through." Or we can choose to say positive words to ourselves, just as my dad made positive statements to that man and other hospital patients. We can choose to say, "Tomorrow's another day." It's up to us. We can allow the Good Shepherd to guide us. The Twenty-third Psalm promised us that he will "lead us beside the still waters."

Learn

The brain is one of the greatest gifts God has given us. It has been estimated that if our human brain were duplicated in a computer today it would cost more than three billion dollars to build and it would take a building the size of the Empire State Building to house it. The entire Mississippi River would be needed to cool the power and energy to run such an enormous machine. Scientists estimate that human beings don't use even a tenth of their brains, which means 90 percent of that God-given gift is lying dormant waiting for us to use it.

More than eighty years ago Dr. William James, a Harvard professor of philosophy and a licensed psychologist, observed, "Compared to what we ought to be, we are only half awake. Our fires are dampened, our drafts are checked. We are making use of only a small part of our mental and physical resources."

No one knows the power of the spirit within each of us. Scientists have not measured it as they measure the brain. But I would guess that our spirits are one hundred times as powerful as our brains. And combined with God's Spirit, the Holy Spirit, our spirits are probably one thousand times more powerful than our minds. We have a unique potential in mind and spirit that most of us never realize.

Jesus promises us, "The Holy Spirit . . . will teach you all things."[5] All things. When you're on your way to success and you run into that brick wall, remember this Scripture. The Holy Spirit will teach you all things.

When the will of our indomitable spirits combines with the intelligence of our minds, all we need for success is the effort to carry out our plans. Thomas Edison was often referred to as a genius, but Edison said he wasn't a genius, just a hard worker. As he explained it, "Genius is two percent inspiration and 98 percent perspiration."

Learning is a way of life for positive people. God wants that way of life for us. Proverbs 4:5 says, "Get wisdom! Get understanding!"

Listen to God speaking by opening your mind to possibility thinking. Learn to use the power of your mind and spirit. Then allow God to lift you out of the valley. Paul told the Romans, "Likewise the Spirit also helps in our weaknesses."[6]

Lift

Birds are lifted by air currents. They can't fly without the air to support them. Yet, when we ponder this miracle, it seems impossible. What do birds fly on? *Air*. And what is air? *An invisible vapor*. You can suck the stuff into your lungs. How then is it possible for a one-hundred-pound condor to fly on it? Aerodynamics aside, flying is a miracle. Similarly, God's ability to lift our spirits out of the valley of depression and up to the mountain peaks is also a miracle. Allow the Good Shepherd to lift you out of your problems, just as all good shepherds lift their sheep to save them from being "cast."

Sheep like to roll over on their backs and rest. But as they are resting, their legs become numb from sticking up in the air, which causes the blood circulation to be cut off. The sheep are "cast" or "cast down." It becomes impossible for them to roll over.

There is nothing a lamb can do. It's helpless. If it's cast down on a warm day, the sheep can die in a matter of a few hours. In moderate temperatures, it may be a few days before it suffocates.

The shepherd counts his sheep so that he will not miss a lamb who might be cast somewhere. He goes out looking for it. Once it is found, he tenderly rolls the sheep over on its side. If the sheep is down for a long time, the shepherd has to lift the sheep onto its feet and then hold it erect and rub its limbs to restore the circulation to its legs.

Phillip Keller, who was once a sheep herder says in his book, *A Shepherd Looks at Psalm 23*, "When I read the life story of Jesus Christ and examine His conduct in coping with human need, I see Him again and again as the Good Shepherd picking up 'cast' sheep."

Robert A. Schuller

Sometimes we get in a rut. We're helpless. But our Shepherd counts his sheep each day. When one is missing, he goes out and looks for the one that hasn't stayed with the herd. He lifts that lamb and massages its legs until the blood begins to surge through its veins. Then the lamb can stand up and walk on its own.

God is ready and eager to guide us and restore our souls. Even in our most depressed times, God can pull our souls out of the valley and put us atop the mountain. Make your prayer, "Guide me, Lord. Lead me beside the still waters and restore my soul." You'll be amazed at how quickly God will respond to your request.

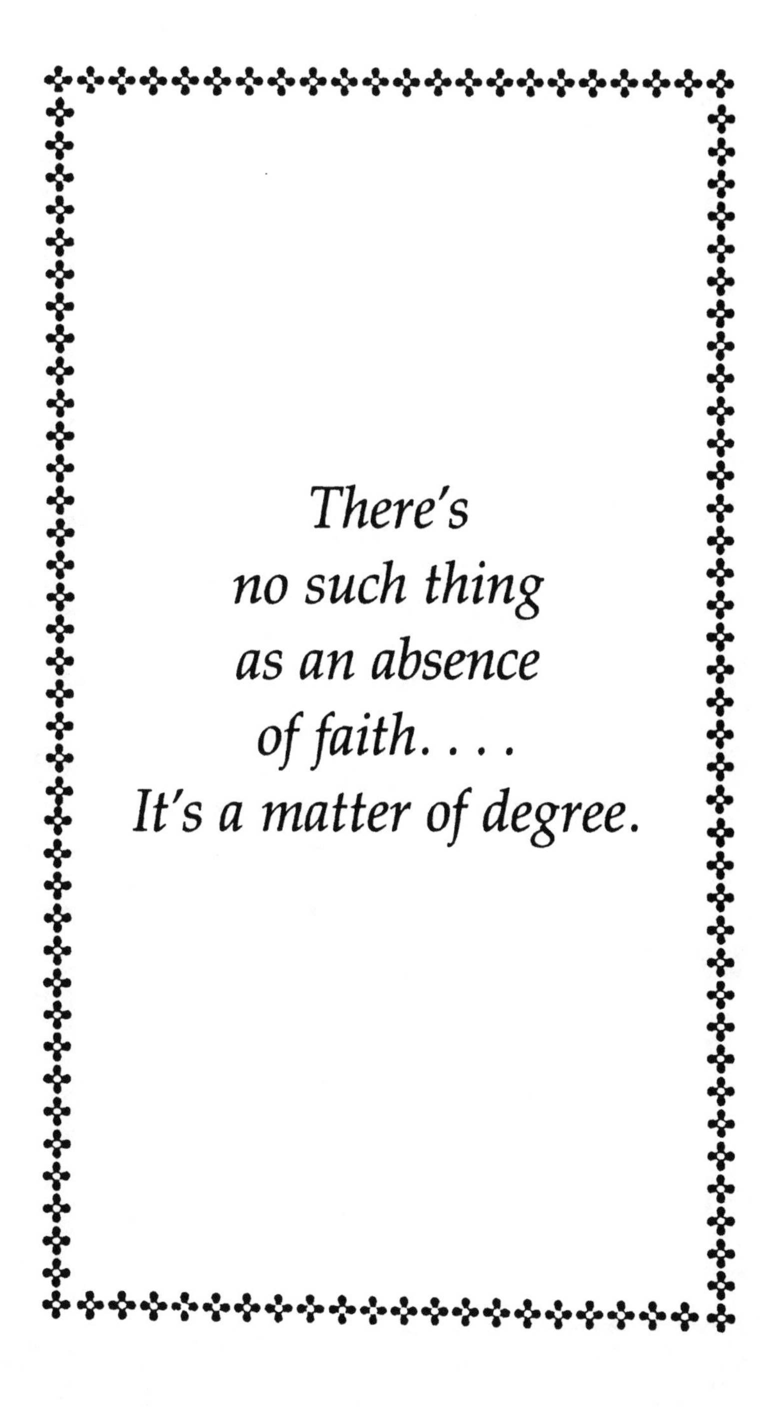

There's
no such thing
as an absence
of faith. . . .
It's a matter of degree.

STEP FOUR

✣ ✣ ✣

Replace Guilt with Gratitude.

"He leads me in the paths of righteousness for his name's sake."

"I feel guilty" is a phrase ministers hear frequently when counseling people who are depressed, worried, and anxious. A feeling of guilt can be overwhelming or just a nagging reminder from our consciences that we've done something wrong.

In 1983 I read an article by a well-known family counselor about the deterioration of family life in America. He had asked fathers to answer the question, "How many hours or minutes do you spend with your one-year-old-child?" The average of all the times mentioned by these men was fifteen to twenty minutes a day.

The counselor then attached a microphone to the children of these fathers and taped their entire day for several days. The average time the children actually spent with their fathers was only ten to fifteen seconds a day!

At the time I read this article, I was already wondering what I might have done to contribute to the failure of my marriage. Had I neglected my family? In the next weeks I worried about this possibility. If I attended evening meetings several nights in a row, I felt guilty about not spending enough time at home. Then, when I deliberately spent time at home, I felt guilty about shirking my work.

Guilt can form an endless cycle of self-remonstration. It gets to the point that no matter what we do, we feel some form of guilt about it. Maybe you're feeling inadequate as a parent. Maybe you feel you have stretched the truth a little too far in order to achieve some personal gains. Maybe you feel you haven't done your best at home, at work, or at school. Perhaps you feel you've missed your mark in life and haven't made much of the time given you.

If you feel this way, then the prayer, "Cleanse me, Lord," is for you. You need to turn to God and pray, "Cleanse me from these negative feelings. Cleanse me from my feelings of guilt."

God is always willing to forgive you. I want to share with you three principles that have helped me to understand God's forgiveness, the silt of guilt, the pace of grace, and the attitude of gratitude.

The Silt of Guilt

Each of us has a God-instilled desire to be perfect because working toward perfection is one of God's purposes for our lives here on earth. Unfortunately, many people think perfection is attainable right here, right now—or at least in the near future. But Scripture teaches that perfection is not attainable here on earth. Therefore, everyone in our world suffers from guilt because no one is perfect. I challenge you to name a perfect human being, even in the Bible.

Consider, for example, the author of Psalm 23, David, a man who did great things for God yet made some large mistakes along the way.

Reasonable Guilt

One evening when David's army was far from Jerusalem besieging the city of Rabbah, David was at home standing on his porch enjoying the view of Jerusalem at dusk. While standing there, he looked into the private courtyard of Uriah, the Hittite. Uriah's lovely wife, Bathsheba, was bathing. Had David been at the battlefront where a warrior king belonged, he would not have been lured by Bathsheba's beauty. Instead he was tempted and sent his messengers to bring Bathsheba to him.

Months later, the young woman sent a message of her own to David: "I'm pregnant."

The great King David was no different from any of us. His first thought was, *How can I cover my sin*? He brought Bathsheba's husband back to Jerusalem so the baby could plausibly be his. But, unlike David, Uriah refused to enjoy the comforts of home while his comrades in the army were enduring the hardships of battle. Uriah slept on David's doorstep with the servants instead of returning to his own bed. Finally, David gave up and asked Joab, Uriah's commander, to place the young man in the forefront of the battle so he would be killed.

As we all know, David broke two of God's commandments: "You shall not kill" and "You shall not commit adultery." David's sins were not small sins. Hopefully many of us will never match his transgressions. Yet God forgave David. Why?

First, because David prayed, "Cleanse me, Lord." When the prophet Nathan confronted David with his sin, the king did not rationalize; he did not lie to himself or to the prophet. David replied, "I have sinned against the Lord."[1] In Psalm 51, written after Nathan's visit, David continued his plea to God, "Create in me a clean heart, O God, and renew a steadfast spirit within me."

Second, David remained faithful in his determination to please God. When Bathsheba's baby died, David could have railed against God. Instead, he humbled himself in acceptance. David faced his sin and truly repented. So, God forgave him.

The silt of guilt can be washed away with the simple prayer, "Cleanse me, Lord. Forgive me for my mistakes and cleanse me from the silt of guilt, which keeps me from being everything I know I can be and from everything you want me to be."

What often holds us back from receiving all the blessings God wants to give us? What often keeps us from receiving the answers to our prayers? Only unforgiven sin.

The good news is that we can always be forgiven. God has said, "If My people who are called by My name will humble themselves, and pray and seek My face, and turn from their wicked ways, then I will hear from heaven, and will forgive their sin and heal their land."[2]

Immediately, not a day or a week or a month or a year later, but the moment after David repented of his sins, the prophet Nathan pronounced absolution. God's forgiveness is just that quick. Bathsheba was soon pregnant again with David's heir, Solomon, whose name means peaceful. To David and Bathsheba, the new baby's birth symbolized that God was at peace with them.

Unsuspected Guilt

David was well aware of his sin, as most of us are when we consciously give in to temptation and disobey one of God's commandments. However, some of us sin and are not aware of it, so we do not seek repentance. The question I have often asked myself is: "What practices does our society condone that cause us to sin without our realizing it?"

Before the Civil War, slave owners in the South blinded themselves to the wrong they were doing. Slavery was a way of life. People kept slaves in biblical times, they reminded themselves. The Bible even condoned slavery, some said, and they proved their point by quoting Ephesians 6: "Slaves, obey your earthly masters with respect and fear, and with sincerity of heart, just as you would obey Christ."[3]

Today, many generations later, we look back at that time and ask, "How could they have possibly treated human beings in that fashion?" What sins are we committing today that our children and grandchildren will one day point a finger at us and ask, "How could you have possibly allowed something like that to go on?"

Each individual must ask that question of himself or herself. God will forgive our mistakes if we face them as David did and truly repent.

Unreasonable Guilt

Some of us feel guilty even though we have not done anything wrong. A clinical psychologist who is a friend of mine says that many of the people he counsels are victims of needless guilt, people who have taken upon themselves guilt that does not belong to them.

Let me tell you the story of one eighteen-year-old girl, whom we will call Laurie. She is an extremely attractive young woman who has a great sense of humor and is essentially well balanced.

The first fourteen years of Laurie's life were quite

normal. She was raised in an upper middle class home, she made good grades in school, and she was fairly popular with her peers. Suddenly, her father went away "to work on a project somewhere else," her mother said. After five months Laurie began to doubt her mother's explanation. Her dad occasionally returned home to see them, but a man always accompanied him and stayed with the family for the few hours her father was there.

After two years her father returned. At first their family life seemed to return to normal. Then her mother, who had been a beautiful woman, became very depressed and began to vent her frustration by fighting with her husband and overeating, which caused her to become extremely heavy. She began to accuse Laurie. "You're responsible for the problems in this family," she told her. "You're away from home all the time. You never help with the housework. No one around here really cares about me."

At the same time, Laurie's dad, whom she had always loved, complained to her, "Your mother is such a witch. She's constantly complaining; I just don't understand her." Laurie became a parent to her parents, constantly trying to resolve the difficulties between them. When she was seventeen, her dad finally told her he had been caught embezzling from his best friend's company.

"I was in prison for those two years I was away. John knew I didn't mean to harm his company. That's why he hired me back when I got out. I really didn't do anything wrong," he assured his daughter.

Laurie could understand how her father's best friend could forgive him and again trust him as a valued employee because everyone seemed to like her dad. He not only was good-looking, he also was very charming. Sometimes Laurie even wondered if her mom was so temperamental because she was jealous of all her husband's friends.

Laurie graduated from high school at seventeen and took a job as a secretary. One night her father picked her up from work. "Want to go dancing with me?" he asked. Laurie enjoyed her father's company. She said yes. Soon after they entered the discotheque, Laurie noticed that she was the only woman there. Men were talking to other men and dancing with other men. Soon Chuck, a good friend of Laurie's dad, came up to their table and asked her dad to dance. On the way home, her dad admitted that he and Chuck had been having an affair for years. "Don't tell your mother or anyone else," her father warned. Now Laurie was truly caught in the web of lies between her parents.

A few months later, Laurie's new boss, a man who was ten years older than she was, invited her to dinner as a thank-you for working some extra hours. Laurie took the invitation at face value and accepted. They ate dinner at an exclusive restaurant and on their way home, he raped her.

"Laurie felt responsible for her parents' problems and responsible for the rape," her counselor told me. "Laurie was a true victim, and, as victims sometimes do, she became involved in an abusive relationship with another man. Victims get into relationships in which they remain victims. They continually allow themselves to be exploited."

When this man finally left her, Laurie sought professional guidance and counseling. She blamed herself for everything: her father's homosexuality, her mother's obesity, the rape, the other man's abuse of her. Yet, if you met her at a party or saw her in public, you would think, *What a golden girl! She's got everything going for her: good looks, charm, intelligence.*

In the first six months of Laurie's therapy, her counselor encouraged her to talk about her problems, which is a healing procedure in itself. Then he began cognitive psychotherapy, which is based on the idea that our thoughts control our feelings and our feelings can control our behavior. The counselor helped Laurie realize that her guilt was unreasonable. She was neither responsible for her mother's depression nor her father's bisexual behavior.

Unfair Judgment

Actually we are judging ourselves when we feel guilty. And the Bible explicitly directs us: "Judge not, and you shall not be judged." It warns, if you do judge others (or yourself), God will judge you in the same way. We have no right to judge ourselves or others improperly. Scripture tells us to leave judgment to God.

You may have blatantly violated one of God's laws, as David did, or you may have made a mistake because it seemed right according to today's standards. Or you may be a victim, like Laurie, and feel guilty even though you have done nothing wrong. If so, I have good news for you. Regardless of your situation, it can be overcome. Communication between you and God can be restored. Pray the simple prayer, "Forgive me, Lord. Cleanse me from the silt of guilt."

A simple prayer of confession washes away the silt of guilt. Have you ever gotten charcoal on your hands when you were cleaning the fireplace? With a little soap and warm water—presto!—the black soot is gone. It's even easier to wash away the ashes of guilt. No soap or water is needed, just the simple prayer, "Cleanse me, Lord. Forgive me."

The Pace of Grace

Psychologist Dr. Chris Knippers, who is a member of our staff at the Rancho Capistrano Community Church, says, "It takes faith to release a feeling of guilt or fear. People can point to one or more specific things that cause them to feel guilty. In order to feel forgiven, they want equally tangible acts of absolution. But it doesn't work like that. It takes faith. And that isn't something that psychologists or ministers can give people. Forgiveness is an act of grace from God. People must have the faith it takes to accept this forgiveness."

Laurie's counselor knew she would have to understand God's grace before she could get over her feelings of guilt, yet she had told him in her first session, "I know you're a Christian. I want to make it clear right now that

I don't want you to try to convert me or anything."

"We won't deal specifically with spiritual principles if you don't want to," the counselor promised. "But remember, Laurie, you're in a process of growth. We'll just see what happens."

In the last six months of her therapy, Laurie started asking questions about God. "Do you really think it helps to talk to him?" she asked.

"Yes, I do," the counselor replied. "But I thought you didn't want to talk about God."

"Well, I've been thinking about religion lately. I've just been wondering."

Laurie's counselor made a suggestion to her that he often gives to someone who feels alienated from God. "Take a walk alone on an isolated part of the beach. Listen to the waves and the birds. If you have any thoughts at all, let them be about God."

Often, through nature, God becomes very evident to people who are not churchgoers. People tell me that when they see and hear the waves rolling in to the shore, they know that there must be some force of power in the universe that is greater than they are.

A few weeks later when Laurie expressed this feeling, her counselor suggested that she start talking to God about how she was feeling. "Don't ask for things, just talk to God the way you talk to me. Then ask him to help you feel his forgiveness." Not too long after that, Laurie began attending a church in her community.

The final phase of Laurie's therapy was to help her to realize all the positive aspects of her personality. As Laurie's self-esteem improved, her relationships began to change. She met a young man at church whose company she enjoyed. She made friends with some of the girls her age. In her last session, she said to her counselor, "You know, I finally believe all the good things you've been telling me about myself. You've told me I'm strong and intelligent, but until recently I couldn't think of myself that way. Now I can."

Laurie's counselor helped her by showing her what a truly amazing person she was. And God gave Laurie the grace to release her guilt and see herself as his child.

Once we have asked for forgiveness, we can return to the path of righteousness with the pace of grace, for no power on earth or in heaven can keep us from the love of God. He loves us so much he gave his son so that whoever believes in him shall not perish but have everlasting life. The pace of God's grace can keep up with the fastest of runners.

Some people feel that Christianity does not offer motivation for living an upright life. They hear about the peace of grace and say, "There's no justice. A person can do whatever he or she wishes since all sin is washed away by the grace of Jesus Christ." They are misunderstanding one of the most basic principles of Christianity: the attitude of gratitude.

An Attitude of Gratitude

In order to get through the going-through stage, you must take the fourth step: eliminate the guilt you feel and then express an attitude of gratitude. Our immense gratitude for God's love and great gift of salvation makes us desire to do everything possible to live up to God's laws. We should be continually grateful to God for his grace and mercy.

In Mark Twain's novel, *Tom Sawyer*, there is a chapter in which Tom is lost at night and hears wild animals coming near him. Tom prays fervently to God that if he will rescue him from this danger, Tom will spend the rest of his life in Sunday school. When the wild animals turn out only to be dogs leading a rescue party to find him, Tom quickly forgets his pledge to God and falls back into his old habits.

Tom Sawyer is typical of many people. Whenever we are in stressful situations, we are willing to pledge ourselves to God and to praise him for his goodness. When the stress passes, however, we ignore God and go our own way.

Others like Mary Nemec Doremus are continually thankful for God's blessings to them despite the difficulties they face each day. They live their lives in an attitude of gratitude.

Mary was born in New York City. She says she inherited her creativity from her mother who was a coproducer for CBS and also wrote the radio show "Suspense." Her stamina, she says, she inherited from her father. Her family—seven children and her parents—moved to Palm Beach, Florida, and Mary grew up playing on the beach. Her dream was to be an actress and by the time she was twenty she was one of the hostesses of the NBC radio show, "Monitor," and had her own television show, "Nightlife on the Gold Coast," on which she interviewed many well-known people, everyone from Bob Hope to Billy Graham.

Her parents were seeing less and less of her, so in 1968 they suggested that she go with them on a family vacation. "Let's go back to our roots," her father suggested. His Czechoslovakian ancestors had been gamekeepers for the king, so they decided to make a trip to Czechoslovakia.

Unfortunately Mary and her family were staying in a hotel on Wenceslaus Square when the Russians invaded. The first warning of the invasion was the tremendous explosion that destroyed the radio and television station. Mary was still working for "Monitor," so she rushed out into the square to see what was happening and to interview anyone who would talk to her. She knew the risk she was taking. As Mary says, "I knew no one would ask me, 'Are you an American?' and then say, 'If you are, I'm not going to shoot you.' "

In the next hours Mary saw men, women, and children being blown apart. She watched as the young man who was standing on the pedestal of King Wenceslaus's statue, holding the Czechoslovakian flag, was shot to death and saw his compatriot pick it up and hold it high. In the next few minutes that young man was killed and another solider took the flag. That flag was passed from soldier to soldier in the next hour, but it never fell to the ground.

Mary watched Russian tanks block the way of the

ambulance that tried to enter the square to get the dying young men to a hospital. "My country had never meant as much to me before that moment," Mary says. "I became very committed to my country and to God."

That night Mary and her family lay on the floor of their room in the hotel with mattresses over their heads. Tracer bullets ricocheted off the walls above them. One verse of Scripture kept going through Mary's mind: "Let the words of my mouth and the meditation of my heart be acceptable in Your sight, O LORD, my strength, and my redeemer."[4]

"I realized that I could lose my life and I could do nothing, absolutely nothing, about it," Mary says. "I knew that I had to get my life in order. I had to understand what I was all about and what my faith really meant to me. 'What is my life worth to me?' I asked myself. 'What is it worth to others?'

"Suddenly, it didn't seem so important to see my name in lights. I realized that the passage of Scripture that kept running through my head was all that was really important. I wanted my life to be valuable in God's eyes. I wanted to help put other people's names in lights. That night I knew that I would do anything to live and make my life count."

Mary and her family finally made it over the border to West Germany, where she was immediately interviewed by a team from the Huntley-Brinkley show. In the next year she spoke throughout the United States, challenging young people to appreciate the freedom they took for granted.

Ten years later, Mary's family took another family vacation to fulfill a promise her father had made to the children during their escape from Czechoslovakia. "If we get across the border," her father had said, "we'll do something very special together ten years from now."

In 1978, the nine members of the Nemec family joined the first visitors to China. But again tragedy struck. When they returned, Mary realized she had contracted some kind of illness in China. For a year, intense pain, nausea, and a low-grade fever plagued her body. She visited doctor after doctor. None of them seemed to know what was wrong with her. "You're beautiful. You seem to be in good health," they said. "Are you happy at home?" Mary knew the doctors were implying that her symptoms were psychosomatic. Day after day, she prayed, *Lord, help the doctors to know what's wrong with me.*

"Again I looked for a purpose in what was happening to me," Mary says. "I prayed, 'What do you want from me, Lord?'

"Finally, I gave up the need to know what my illness was," Mary said. "That was the healthiest thing that ever happened to me. I accepted what was, and then I moved on with what could be."

Three years later Mary became limp-paralyzed; her body was as uncontrollable as a rag doll's. Because of her extreme muscle weakness, she had to use a wheel chair most of the time. Still Mary tried to turn this new obstacle into an opportunity. "I kept switching careers," she says, "according to what my body could stand."

When her hometown paper, *The Palm Beach Mirror*, asked her to write a column from Washington, "Washington Mary-Go-Round," she immediately said yes. In 1981 she was able to get an interview with the Reagan Inaugural Committee through a friend's influence.

"After fifteen minutes, the people I was interviewing began interviewing me. One of them was Jean Bergaust, the director of the Seniors' Handicapped Committee. She asked me to be a member of their advisory board and to attend a meeting that evening," Mary remembers. "At the meeting I volunteered to raise the funds for an inaugural reception for the handicapped, even though the inauguration was only two weeks away."

Mary spent the next days lying on a couch in the First Aid Room of Inaugural Headquarters, calling businesses and private citizens and personal friends. "Hi, I'm Mary Doremus," she said. "I'm a beautiful blond in a wheel chair."

When Mary became too weak to continue, the nurse helped her into bed. After a short rest, she was back on the phone. In just two weeks she raised twelve thousand dollars for a reception for the disabled (which was also attended by Virginia Mayo, Jimmy Stewart, Erma Bombeck, Ginger Rogers, Nancy Reagan, and Senator Robert Dole), the first opportunity for citizens with disabilities to be an official part of a presidential inauguration.

The day after the reception Mary went into the hospital for tests, but she refused to stay because, as she explained it, "I didn't have time to be sick." The International Year of Disabled Persons had put her on their board and asked her to serve as the special assistant to the president. That year she began the National Challenge Committee on Disability to inspire individuals with handicaps to take an active role in life and to challenge employers and the nation to give the disabled more opportunities to increase their productivity and self-sufficiency.

Just as the program was beginning to gain momentum, Mary became totally dysfunctional. Her doctors suspected that she had a brain lesion and decided to "take her totally out of the world in order to give her body an opportunity to rejuvenate." Mary spent the next eleven months alone in a house in Indianapolis near the Indiana University Medical Center.

"Even though every move was difficult, I took total care of myself. Sometimes I had to inch across the floor on my belly to get to the bathroom. Dr. Schuller's 'Inch by inch, everything's a cinch' became my motto. Inch by inch, I was determined to keep going and get better."

Mary was taking so much prednisone that she gained almost one hundred pounds, which made movement even more difficult. "I felt that I was the ugliest monster in the world. I was huge."

Then Mary began to question her faith. "I put Jesus on hold," she says. "I thought I was alone. I thought I was broken. Yet I wanted to make that dark experience count for something. I kept fighting. I screamed 'Let go and let God' so many times that I was finally able to live those words again. I learned to rejoice in what I can do and stop crying over what I can't do. I learned again to have an attitude of gratitude.

"When I go back through the diaries I kept during this time, I see *Jesus* and *God* written in every entry," Mary says. "I wasn't alone during those days, I just thought I was.

"No one chooses to become disabled," Mary says, "but disability can be a positive experience. Your life can become greater rather than lesser. That's what I try to tell my brothers and sisters with disabilities."

The doctors have found a medication that relieves Mary's paralysis—as long as she takes it every twenty minutes to two hours, depending on her energy level. They now believe that Mary may have an intracranial vasculitis. Throughout each night of her life Mary wakes up over and over again to take her medication. But as she says, "From this affliction, from this bended knee, comes the greatest standing I've ever done." Despite her illness Mary has continued to spearhead the work of the National Challenge Committee on Disability.

"We're changing the way America perceives individuals with disabilities," Mary says. "We're not childlike and dependent, but we're strong. What we look or sound like has nothing to do with what we are able to do. When you see me sitting in my wheel chair, the last thing I want you to notice is my disability. The first thing I want you to notice is my abilities."

At a time when her illness is at its worst, Mary is making her greatest contribution. Through most of her illness she has maintained an attitude of gratitude. She has continually struggled to find a purpose in what is happening to her. She continually fights to make her life count. She is continually grateful to God for his grace and mercy.

If you are feeling down and out, overcome your negative thoughts. Pray the prayer, "Cleanse me, Lord." Accept the pace of grace. Then express an attitude of gratitude for the blessings God has in mind for you. Your finest hour will grow out of your greatest burden. With God, all things are possible.

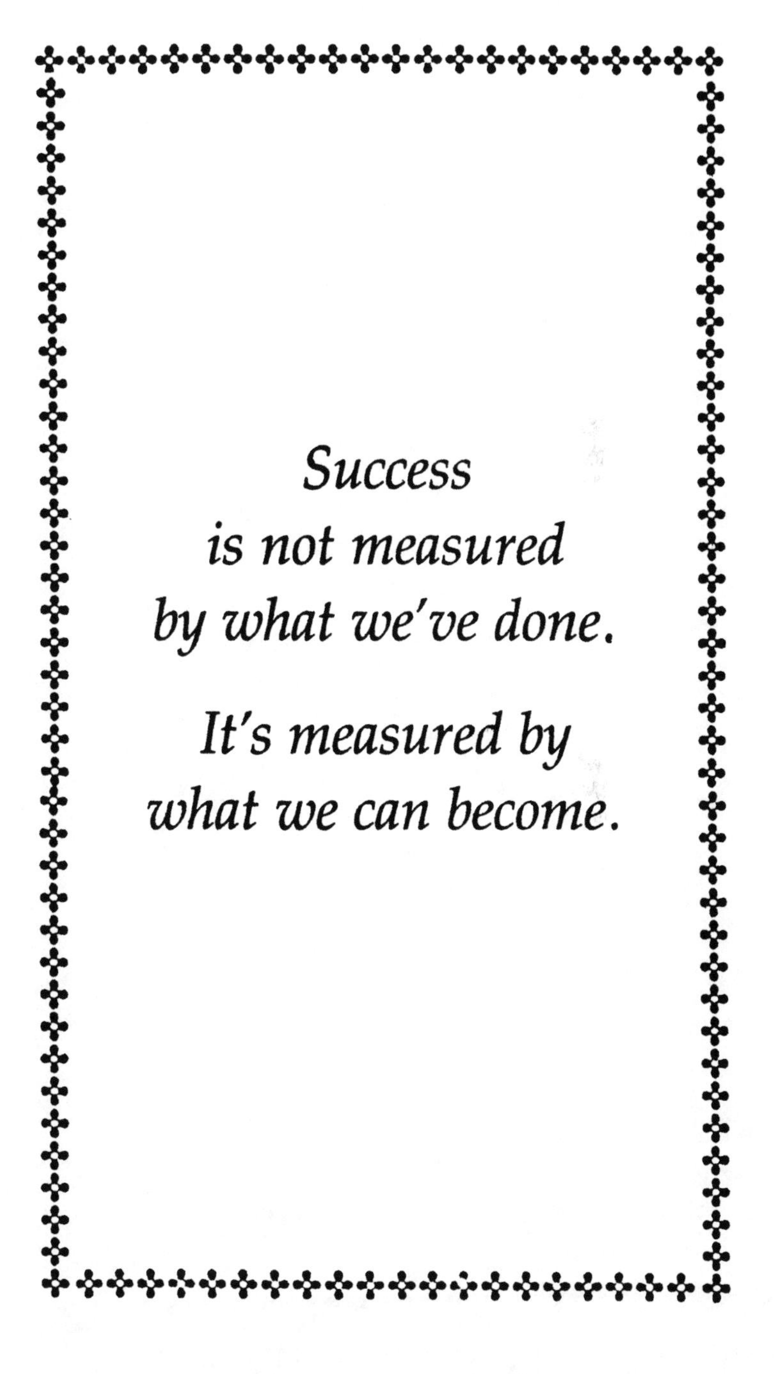

Success
is not measured
by what we've done.

It's measured by
what we can become.

STEP FIVE

✣ ✣ ✣

Face Your Fears with Faith.

"Yea, though I walk through the valley of the shadow of death, I will fear no evil."

The most difficult period of my life took place at a time that should have been the most exciting. The doors of the Rancho Capistrano Community Church were to open in September of 1983. I had also been nominated to sit on the international board of the Robert Schuller Ministries. Many goals for my life were being fulfilled, except for one: a happy family life. I realized that my marriage was dissolving.

Early in the summer of 1983 I began to notice that Linda wasn't wearing her wedding ring. I confronted her a couple of times and she answered, "I forgot it. No big deal. Don't worry about it."

She had started going to a psychologist during the previous year because she was feeling depressed. By July she told me she wanted a divorce. At first I didn't take her seriously. I'd heard that statement several times during the first year of our marriage, nine years earlier.

This time, however, she persisted. Finally, I said, "That isn't an option. There are several other options that could help us work this out. One would be to see a marriage counselor together. But divorce is not one of those options.

"Marriage is an institution," I went on, "and once you make a commitment to it, you stick it out and make it work." I'd given the same advice in a much more subtle manner to the couples I had counseled in premarital classes or those who had come to me to discuss marital difficulties.

Linda continued to express her dissatisfaction with our marriage in the next weeks, so I suggested that we see if a counselor could help us. During our first counseling session, the possibility seemed remote. The counselor asked Linda, "Do you want this marriage to work?" and she answered, "No."

The counselor suggested that we draw up a contract

to work out our problems, each of us listing a few items that we felt were critical to a good relationship. Linda wanted more freedom, she said, social freedom to go out at night with her own friends and financial freedom to spend money as she desired. I asked that we try to develop a more loving and intimate relationship and that she call to let me know she was all right whenever she was out late.

The contract lasted about two months; then, early in September Linda suddenly announced that she was going to spend ten days with her cousin in the Midwest. I was extremely angry. That coming Sunday leaders from our denomination, the Reformed Church in America, the oldest Protestant ministry in the United States, were coming to dedicate our new church. To me, her absence at such an important celebration would be a public declaration that our marriage was failing.

I went to see the counselor by myself that week. "What am I to do now?" I asked in desperation after telling her why I was alone.

"Why not write a letter to Linda and explain to her how you feel? Tell her what you want in a marriage relationship," she suggested.

It didn't take Linda long to respond to my letter. Even though I couldn't see her face, her voice sounded shrill when I answered the telephone. "No way, there's no way I can possibly fulfill the things you want of me," she said almost immediately. She returned home a week later, but we didn't see each other very much after that. In the daytime I was gone, and after dinner if I wasn't at a church function, she was gone for the evening.

In spite of this, the counselor requested that we remain together until after the holidays, just to make sure that Linda really wanted a divorce and to be doubly sure that a decision to end the relationship was right. Those were three of the most excruciating months I have ever spent. I felt as if I couldn't share the burden with anyone, not even my family, for fear that if I admitted our problems to anyone else, all hope for reconciliation would be jeopardized. For the first time in my life I dreaded the holidays. For my marriage, they signified the end.

I'll never forget that Christmas Day, the last holiday we spent together as a family. Each time I picked up the children and held them, I realized I wouldn't be able to hold and kiss them each day. I wouldn't be able to hear their prayers each night. I would no longer be a part of their everyday lives.

The day after Christmas was even worse. I came downstairs in the morning and picked up my daughter, Angie, to hug her. Tears came to my eyes and the knot in my stomach tightened, making me feel physically sick. I had to put her down and run to the bathroom as I could not control my emotions. I'd begin to enjoy playing with Angie and her brother, Bobby, and then I'd realize in a few days we would be separated. My throat would tighten, my stomach would feel queasy, and I'd begin to choke. The ache I felt was so deep that I couldn't stand it anymore. I went off to a friend's condominium in Laguna Beach the next day.

When I returned a week later, I was ready to agree with Linda. "We can't go on this way," I admitted. "Let's either get back together or let's file for divorce." I knew her answer before she said it: "Let's file for divorce."

That Friday, January 6, we went to an attorney, and on Sunday I began to preach the series of messages, "Getting through the Going-through Stage." I concluded my first sermon with this story, which may be familiar to you but is worth repeating because it gives a new perspective to getting through the going-through stage.

Footprints in the Sand

One night a man had a dream. He dreamed he was walking along the beach with the Lord. Across the sky flashed scenes from his life. For some scenes, he noticed two sets of footprints in the sand: one belonging to him, and the other to the Lord.

When the last scene of his life flashed before

him, he looked back at the footprints in the sand. Many times along the path of his life there had been only one set of footprints. He noticed that it happened at the very lowest and saddest times in his life.

This really bothered him so he questioned the Lord about it. "Lord, you said that once I decided to follow you, you'd walk with me all the way. But I have noticed that during the most troublesome times in my life, there is only one set of footprints. I don't understand why when I needed you most you left me."

The Lord replied, "My precious, precious child, I love you and I would never leave you. During your times of trial and suffering, when you saw only one set of footprints, it was then that I carried you."

During those early months of 1984, I often reread "Footprints" and prayed the prayer, "Carry me, Lord. Carry me so that I can walk through the valley of the shadow of death. Carry me so I can face my fear of what lies ahead."

The fifth step in getting through the going-through stage is: face your fears with faith, just as David did on that miraculous day when he killed the giant Goliath. Facing problems, I've found, can be God's way of guiding us toward greater strength and, eventually, to bigger goals than we ever dreamed possible.

Face Your Fears with Faith

Despite the swaggering, gigantic figure of Goliath, whose armor alone weighed 225 pounds, the young shepherd, David, lived the words of his psalm: "Though I walk through the valley of the shadow of death, I will fear no evil." He faced his fear by applying four positive principles:

- Have vision
- Have faith
- Put your faith into action
- Allow God to carry you

Some of us are facing problems of incredible magnitude; we, too, have our Goliaths. I know people who are fighting cancer. That's a Goliath. I know people who are fighting to save their marriages, as I was. That's a Goliath. Some people are facing an even greater Goliath, the Goliath of unbelief, the Goliath of negative thinking: "I can't do that."

Consider David's Goliath, the giant of the Philistines, a man who was raised as a warrior, probably sold to the government at the age of five because of his strong stature, and trained for years as a warrior and professional killer. Goliath, we're told, was six cubits and a span, which experts calculate to be at least nine feet, six inches tall. Imagine his size. Wilt Chamberlain is even short compared to Goliath.

Now imagine what David faced the day he took provisions to his brothers. Each army was encamped on a mountain on the opposite sides of the valley of Elah. Every morning and every evening for forty days Goliath stood in front of the Israelites and mocked them. Eighty times Goliath challenged a member of the Israelite army to meet him in mortal combat. Eighty times there was no answer. The entire army of Israel was "dismayed and greatly afraid."[1] They were shaking in their boots.

How did David respond to Goliath's challenge? He didn't shake and quiver. He immediately had a vision of success: "I believe I can conquer Goliath," he said.

Have Vision

To overcome your Goliath, you first must have a vision. "I believe I can conquer my mountain. I believe I can do the impossible."

In 1981 when I got the vision for the Rancho Capistrano Community Church I shared it with my dad. What was his response?

"But, Robert, it's not like it used to be!"

No one loves me any more than my parents do, but my dad's response was far from positive. Critics—and sometimes even loved ones who wish us the best—may try to dim our vision.

David got the idea: I believe I can succeed. He held on to that vision despite negative comments. "What on earth are *you* doing here?" was the gist of his brother's reaction when David arrived at the camp.

What a slap in the face! "You're just a shepherd," Eliab reminded him. He told him to get out of the way and to go back to the sheep. He accused him of just coming to the front in order to see the battle. "Who do you think you are anyway? A soldier?"

When David expressed his vision to others in the crowd, they replied with the same derision. Finally, the word came to Saul: believe it or not there's one fool who is willing to fight the giant. Immediately Saul called David into his tent and warned him, "You are not able to go against this Philistine to fight with him, for you are but a youth."[2]

Everywhere he turned, David met with criticism. "You can't do that.... You can't succeed.... Who do you think you are anyhow?"

To overcome your Goliath, you must be able to face criticisms and ignore negative comments. I've coined a tongue twister to remind me of this principle: "A fighter full of faith always conquers his fears and foes and makes his future a fantastic, fruitful friend."

David had a vision. He ignored his brother's negative criticism. His objective was to convince Saul that he could kill Goliath, since the future of the entire nation of Israel depended on David's success. Goliath had said, "If one of your men can kill me, then we will be your servants. But if I prevail, then you shall be our servants."

David did not tell Saul how many men he had killed, since he had never fought a mortal battle with another human being. He did not brag about the years he had spent in the army, since he had never had military training. Instead David said, "The LORD, who delivered me from the paw of the lion and from the paw of the bear, He will deliver me from the hand of this Philistine."[3]

Have Faith in Your God-given Ability

To lose is not a sin, but to give up is a tragedy. Saul could not argue with David's logic. Alone David had little chance, as Saul had already pointed out. But with the almighty, omnipotent God at David's side, Saul could not predict what would happen. Their God was the God who had parted the Red Sea, the God who had led the Israelite armies when they conquered the Promised Land. Who could say what this young shepherd could do if God was truly at his side?

To overcome your Goliath, you must have faith in God and in the ability he has given you. Together you can conquer any mountain.

Put Your Faith into Action

You can talk about your faith, you can sell your ability, you can have all the faith in the world, but until your faith is put into action, you will never win the battle.

David killed the giant. He faced his Goliath and he won and he left no doubt as to why. David knew he had an unseen Power at his side. No matter how weak or ineffective we may feel, like David we have large wings under our little wings, unlike a little bird my daughter, Angie, adopted as a pet.

One day Angie was visiting my mom and dad and noticed a sparrow's nest underneath the overhang by their front door. For weeks she watched as the sparrows hatched and then squeaked for food from the safety of their nest. Finally, one of the sparrows flew out of the nest. Angie watched as the tiny bird flew around and around and finally landed in the pond in the front yard. Before my parents could get the bird out of the water, it drowned.

"Poor little bird," Angie said, "he didn't know his wings were too little to fly. He just didn't know his wings were too weak to fly."

We have large wings under our little wings. We have strong hands under our weak hands. We have a God who loves us and cares about us and wants us to succeed. He promises that "those who wait on the LORD shall renew their strength; they shall mount up with wings like eagles, they shall run and not be weary, they shall walk and not faint."[4]

In the summer of 1984, Steve McWhorter, the Episcopal priest I mentioned in the first chapter, went to the island of Mykonos, Greece, in the Mediterranean Sea to rest and write. One day he jumped on his mo-ped to go to the beach. He was cruising along at ten miles per hour when he hit a stone. Steve was thrown off and the bike landed on his left leg. Once he regained his senses, Steve realized he could hardly move because of the pain in this leg.

Not too long after the accident a small car full of four Yugoslavian students drove up. They managed to squeeze Steve in the back of the car and set out to find a doctor. They drove up to one house with a red cross on it only to discover that the doctor had died a week earlier.

About an hour later they drove up to another doctor's house. The doctor sewed up the large laceration on Steve's arm and one on his leg. Then he felt Steve's leg and arm for any broken bones.

"Your leg is severely bruised, but it is not broken," he admitted to Steve.

The pain in Steve's leg told him different. "Can we x-ray my leg just to make sure?"

"There is no x-ray equipment on the island," the doctor admitted. "But your leg will be okay. Just keep it elevated."

Steve could hardly walk out of the doctor's office that day. The excruciating pain in his leg made it impossible to put any weight on it. He was sure the leg was broken. He could not ignore the negative circumstance in which he found himself. He had tears in his eyes as he rode to his hotel in a taxi. Once he was back in his room, lying on the bed, his leg throbbing with pain, Steve wondered, *What am I going to do next*?

The words of Isaiah 40 came into his mind: "Those who wait on the Lord shall renew their strength; they shall mount up with wings like eagles."

"I began to scratch my head," Steve says, "and say, 'Steve, why on earth are you worrying at all. Why are you doubting as Peter did? Where is your faith? The Lord will bear you up on eagle's wings.' "

Steve McWhorter had a vision of help. He ignored the negatives. He renewed his faith. Then he put the vision into action. He called some friends he had met on the island, and they took him to the airport for a flight in a tiny plane to Athens.

Jetways are unknown at the Athens airport. So Steve next faced the steps of a jumbo jet bound for London, which he said, "looked like Mt. Kilimanjaro" to him because of the pain in his leg.

The flight attendant had noticed his agonizing limp. "You think you can get up those steps?" he asked.

"Only on my fanny," Steve replied.

"You can't do that," the attendant exclaimed. He took Steve to the food elevator and loaded him on.

In London Steve was put into a wheelchair and taken to the dispensary where he asked the nurse, "Do you know of a good orthopedic hospital in or near Paddington?" He had some good friends in this area.

The nurse smiled. "The finest orthopedic hospital in London is in Paddington. It's called St. Mary's."

By the next day, Steve's leg had been "bolted back together with a compression plate and five pins."

What supported him in Mykonos and what continued to support him throughout that painful trip were the words from Isaiah 40: "Those who wait on the Lord shall renew their strength; they shall mount up with wings like eagles."

McWhorter had a vision. He ignored the negatives. He renewed his faith. Then he put his faith into action. He overcame his Goliath.

God wants you to overcome your Goliath, too. You can do it, just as Steve McWhorter did, just as David, the shepherd boy, did. Pray the prayer, "Carry me, Lord. Carry me so that I will fear no evil." Then rest in God's hands. Picture him carrying you through the valley as he carried the writer of "Footprints in the Sand." God cannot carry you if you don't give your problem over to him completely and allow yourself to be carried.

Allow Yourself to Be Carried

I remember a time when I was not willing to be carried. It was a tradition in my college fraternity to dump each brother into Lake Michigan if he became engaged. It didn't matter what time of the year it was, which was unfortunate for me since I became engaged in February of my sophomore year. You can imagine how cold it was in Holland, Michigan, where Hope College is located. There was no way I was going to be dunked in those icy waters if I could help it.

One night about twenty guys came into the fraternity house looking for me. Fortunately, I was a varsity wrestler and was able to break through the gang and get out of the house. They couldn't carry me because I wasn't willing.

But the next time the brothers were prepared; they lured me into the back seat of a car, wedged me between two other guys, and told me we were going to the grocery store for our weekly shopping. The next thing I knew we were driving down the nearest pier, with two other cars behind us. The guys piled out of the other cars and formed a human wall that led straight to the water. There was no way out! I didn't want to be carried, but I got carried anyway.

To get through the going-through stage you must be willing to be carried and that takes trusting enough to let go and to let God support you. I demonstrated this principle once during a children's sermon. As the children were seated around me waiting to hear the story, I asked several of them if they would allow me to pick them up. The new children looked apprehensive, and a few of them got up enough courage to shake their heads no. It was all right for their moms and dads to pick them up and carry them, but not me.

Why? They didn't know whether or not they could trust me. But they knew they could trust their parents because they had lived with them every day; they had long-term relationships on which to base their trust.

Trust takes that kind of relationship. Do you know God that well? I've learned that getting to know God takes the same amount of time and effort that it takes to get to know anyone. We must talk to him in prayer. We must listen to what he says to us through his words in the Bible. If not, we won't be able to trust him to carry us through the going-through stage.

Remember that old story of the man who fell off a cliff and managed to grab hold of a small tree on the rim? As he hung there, he looked up and screamed, "Is anyone up there who can help me?"

There was silence.

So he yelled again, "Please, is there anyone up there?"

Soon a voice thundered from the sky. "I am here."

"Who are you?" the man asked.

"I am your Lord, the great I Am, your God."

"Is that really you, Lord?" the man yelled.

"Yes."

"Save me, Lord," the man cried.

"I will save you," God said. "Just let go."

The man thought for a moment. Then he replied, "Is there anyone else up there?"

It takes a lot of faith to let go and let the hand of God lift you, but you can't feel God's power until you do. You have to pray the prayer, "Carry me, Lord," then relax in God's arms and feel him carrying you.

There's a party game that youth pastors often have teenagers play. Although it's a game, it teaches the teenagers an important lesson about life, too. The game begins by having one teen stand in the middle of a seven- or eight-foot long two-by-four that is lying on the floor. The teen is then blindfolded. After that, two strong boys get on each end of the plank. The game's director announces that the boys are going to lift the plank five feet off the ground and that the blindfolded person may try to keep his balance.

At that point, the two boys lift the plank a mere two inches off the ground, but they jiggle the board slightly and they grunt and groan as though they are straining to lift the board very high. The blindfolded person begs to be let down. He gets scared and becomes afraid of hitting his head on the ceiling or of falling to the floor. He wants to remove the blindfold, but he must wave his arms in order to keep his balance.

Soon, the blindfolded person calls out for help. At that point, the game director walks over, picks up the person, and sets him safely on the ground. Everyone in the room bursts out with laughter. When the contestant removes his blindfold, he sees that he never was in any danger. His fears had all been imaginary. He had made himself believe his situation was treacherous when in reality he was in no danger. Because he lacked faith in his ability to control the unknown, he had been terrified until he allowed the game director to carry him to safety.

Exercise your faith, allow God to carry you, and face your fears with faith. It's part of a blessed cycle.

The Blessed Cycle

God carries us to the point where we're back on our feet again; then, we're able to reach out to others and carry them when they need a hand. It's a continuous, blessed cycle. Carry and be carried. Be carried and carry. The cycle goes on and on.

A year after my divorce, my father said to me, "You have good judgment, but I have always worried about your sincerity. How could you preach to broken hearts if yours had never been broken? Now you have earned your credentials to preach to people who are hurting."

Dad was right. I can relate to other people's sorrow now that I have gone through a very deep valley of my own.

Robert A. Schuller

The fourth verse of the Twenty-third Psalm always reminds me of the lyrics of the great song, "Higher Ground":

> I'm pressing on the upward way,
> New heights I'm gaining every day,
> Still praying as I'm onward bound,
> "Lord plant my feet on higher ground."
>
> Lord, lift me up and let me stand
> By faith on heaven's table land,
> A higher plane than I have found.
> Lord, plant my feet on higher ground.

When you feel you can't go on, pray the prayer, "Carry me, Lord." When you feel your arms are too tired and your legs are too weak, pray, "Carry me, Lord. Send your spirit, Lord, to fill my sails with your power." Slowly, but surely, you'll be raised to higher ground.

Why me, Lord?

Try me, Lord.

STEP SIX

✣ ✣ ✣

Let Love Lighten Your Load.

"For you are with me."

I met Dr. Gerald Jampolsky, the author of *Goodbye to Guilt* and *Love Is Letting Go of Fear*, in the early spring of 1984. Jerry was near San Juan Capistrano on business and agreed to meet me at his motel. We sat by the swimming pool for several hours, enjoying the warm sun.

Only nine years earlier, Jerry, a successful psychiatrist, had gone through a painful divorce. In the months afterward, he had begun drinking heavily and had developed a chronic, disabling back pain. Finally Jerry had turned to God to seek answers to his problems, after having lived most of his adult life as a militant atheist.

As Jerry and I began to talk about some of the personal things I was going through, particularly my divorce, Jerry told me that his divorce had led him to search for truth. "What do you think truth is, Robert?" he asked me.

I was not really sure how to answer his question.

He saw my hesitancy and said, "Let's put it another way. Can truth change?"

Again I hesitated. Then I said, "No." But I was still not sure where Jerry was headed.

Finally he said, "What is the one source that does not change?"

"God," I answered.

"And what is God?"

"Love."

"Yes, God and love are the only truths that exist, and that's exactly what I found out. I was more surprised than anyone else when I began to think about words like *God* and *love*. I had been extremely judgmental toward people who were religious. I saw them as fearful and I believed they were not using their intellect properly.

"I realized that we are always expressing either fear or love. By choosing love more consistently than fear, I found that I could change the nature and quality of my relationships.

"The next step was to learn to forgive others for the harm I thought they had caused me. Most of us harbor grudges deep down inside. Pictures of experiences that have hurt us play on the screen of our subconscious, influencing everything we do."

He paused to take a drink of water and then continued. "These images are superimposed not only on each other but also on the lens through which we experience the present. Consequently, we are never really seeing or hearing life as it is; we are just seeing the present through the tons of repeated fragments of distorted old memories. They are like old rerun movies that seem new to our conscious selves.

"If we are willing, we can use positive imaging to wipe away everything from those old reels except love. This requires letting go of our past attachments to guilt and fear."

In the next twenty minutes, Jerry took me through an exercise to help me forgive those who I felt had hurt me.

He began by saying, "Whenever I determine that someone else is guilty, I am reinforcing my own sense of guilt and unworthiness. I cannot forgive myself unless I am willing to forgive others.

"Robert, what are the things you feel guilty about?"

At first I couldn't think of much. But Jerry encouraged me to remember anything about which I felt even the slightest twinge of guilt.

"How about your parents? Do you have any guilt in relation to them?"

I thought about my mom and one particular argument we had had. Although I couldn't remember what we were fighting about, I remembered how angry we had become. Finally Mom slapped me, and I was so angry that I slapped her back. It was the only time my mother slapped me and the only time I ever hit my mother.

"I feel guilty about that," I admitted to Jerry.

"What about your father?"

I thought a while and then remembered a similar incident with him. One night I wanted to go out, but my father didn't want me to leave. Again I couldn't remember why we were fighting, just how upset we had both become.

"I'm going," I had insisted.

"No, you're not," he had replied as he moved to stand in the doorway so I couldn't leave. The old saying, "When an irresistible force meets an immovable object, something's got to give," applied here. My advancement was met by my father's resistance.

"Anyone else?" Jerry asked.

I knew he was probably wondering what my feelings were toward Linda. He'd been through a divorce himself and had known the feelings of resentment and guilt. I admitted to him that deep down inside I felt I must have done something to cause Linda to want to divorce me. Yes, I felt guilty. After all, most of us admit that it takes two to fight and that usually there's fault on both sides in a situation like a divorce.

As I admitted in the beginning of chapter four, I felt guilty about the way I had spent my time. Had I neglected my family for my responsibility to the church? I knew that ministers were sometimes guilty of this.

One Episcopal study of clergy divorce observed, "Most lay people are constantly being exhorted not to become workaholics and neglect family relationships. But clergy are encouraged to put their work first and are rewarded for being omnipresent and giving of themselves selflessly when called upon."[1]

I did not admit this guilt to Jerry that day. I did, however, admit my bitterness to him. "I resent her coming into my life, allowing me to love her, and then leaving me nine years later."

Jerry nodded. It was sufficient that, at this point, I was at least able to admit that much about my feelings toward Linda. I was making progress.

Allow Yourself to Feel God's Love

As I've described this conversation between Jerry and me, maybe you have thought of some guilt or resentment you, too, have hidden. Maybe you've hurt someone by your actions. Maybe something has happened between you and your parents. Or you and your spouse. Or you and your children.

Read through this exercise with me now; then, do it by yourself later.

Close your eyes. Imagine that you can see a tiny cell from your heart under a very high-powered microscope. You are looking inside your soul and seeing this cell. It's a very round cell. It's a loving cell.

Now the cell is beginning to radiate with light because that cell is a part of God and it radiates with love. The cell is penetrating through your other cells. It's consuming your entire heart. Soon you are entirely illuminated by love.

The light spreads to your family. Your friends. Your community. Now it's everywhere.

Into this light of love step your mother and your father and any person from whom you are separated by guilt. Through this light steps Jesus, and you and he are one in love. The guilt is gone. It has been washed away through the blood of Jesus Christ and you have been purified through him.

As I sat in a lounge chair beside the pool that morning, the warmth of the sun relaxing my body, I felt God's love and forgiveness as I never had before. I was relaxed. I was at peace. I felt as if I had been let out of jail. Suddenly I had the freedom to go into the office when I wanted to go, to be with my family when I wanted to be with them, to spend time the way I wanted to spend time and not feel guilty about it. Even now as I write these words, I have never felt that guilt again.

I also felt that my self-esteem had been renewed. I think anyone who has had a marriage partner ask for a divorce has felt rejected. We feel as if we are unworthy. The sixth step in getting through the going-through stage is: let love lighten your load by loving yourself. To do this, I rely on positive prayer. Positive prayer changes lives.

Robert A. Schuller

Positive Prayer

A prayer I pray in low moments is, "O Lord, give me the self-esteem to believe in myself and a vision to see where you want this child to be. Then give me the faith to carry it through and the wisdom to know I did."

Positive prayer helps build self-esteem. When you look in a mirror, what do you see? Do you see a child of God, a person with beautiful possibilities, with a future, with hope?

I remember getting into an argument with my older sister when I was eight.

"You're a pig!" I screamed when she refused to give me one of my own toys.

My dad heard me. He came into the room and said, "Robert, don't you ever call your sister a pig again."

"But, Dad, she is!" I objected.

"If you call her a pig, Robert, you're calling me a pig, too!"

I had to think about that for a while. I certainly didn't think my dad was a pig.

Dad could tell that I didn't fully understand what he was saying. "Robert, if your sister is a pig, then I'm a pig. She is my child! I can't have a pig for a child unless I'm a pig. When you insult your sister, you're insulting me, too. When you mock or belittle yourself, you're doing the same thing to me. You're my son.

"The same thing is true for you and God or for your brothers and sisters in the human race and God. When you belittle yourself, you're belittling God. When you insult your neighbor, you're insulting God."

I never forgot that lesson.

When you look in the mirror, look beyond the reflection and see the face of Christ. Years ago, a young immigrant girl named Golda Mabovitz attended Fourth Street Grade School in Milwaukee, Wisconsin. She came to school in ragged clothes and had difficulty learning because of her scant knowledge of the English language. Sometimes she wouldn't come to school at all. Her schoolmates teased her. They thought of her as a loser. A nobody. A nothing. We've all known someone like that, someone who was an outcast.

The social workers visited Golda's home and scolded her parents for allowing her to be truant and for not giving her the food and warm clothes she needed. But the Mabovitzes didn't understand what was being said to them since they couldn't speak English.

When this young girl looked in the mirror, all she could see was a failure. But God saw something different. He saw her as she would be. He saw her returning to that school at age seventy. He saw thousands of people, some of whom were the classmates who had ridiculed her, coming to hear a speech by Golda Meir, the prime minister of Israel. Golda Mabovitz Meir.

I Am Somebody

I may be young; I may be old,
But *I am somebody,*
For I am God's Child.

I may be educated; I may be unlettered,
But *I am somebody,*
For I am God's Child.

I may be black; I may be white,
But *I am somebody,*
For I am God's Child.

I may be rich; I may be poor,
But *I am somebody,*
For I am God's Child.

I may be fat; I may be thin,
But *I am somebody,*
For I am God's Child.

I may be married; I may be divorced,
But *I am somebody*,
For I am God's Child.

I may be successful; I may be a failure,
But *I am somebody*,
For I am God's Child.

I may be a sinner; I may be a saint,
But *I am somebody*,
For Jesus is my Savior.
I am God's Child!

—author unknown

When you look in the mirror, what do you see? Do you see yourself as a person with a positive purpose in life who will continue to grow in the years ahead?

Not too long ago "The Hour of Power" offered a gift for those who wrote to the ministry: a special mirror that had these words inscribed on it, *The me I see is the me I'll be*. How do you view yourself?

Remember, the Lord's Prayer says, "Thy will be done." Ask God to show you his vision for your life. Then see yourself as he sees you.

Some of you may be saying, "There's no way God can use me. I'm over the hill. I'm all washed up. It's all passed me now." I knew a man who felt that way. He had spent his entire life developing a beautiful restaurant where people could enjoy his delicious chicken and have a tasty meal. He was a proud man, fairly wealthy in his own right.

He was planning to retire soon and intended to sell his business. Then a bureaucrat in Washington drew a line on a map and changed Highway 75 so that his restaurant was left on a little-traveled road. In two years his wealth had completely vanished. At the age of sixty-five, he was a broken man. He had nothing.

Some people would have screamed at God, "Why, Lord?" But negative prayer is never answered. Instead, successful people pray, "What, Lord?" This prayer says, "I will continue in your Power."

This man got an idea. He began peddling his chicken. He traveled from place to place and started selling franchises of chicken. Today the chain is known as Colonel Sander's Kentucky Fried Chicken.

You may be looking in the mirror today and saying, "I'm all washed up. Everything's gone. There is no chance my marriage can survive. There is no chance my business can come out of this recession. There is no chance that God can change my life." But God loves you and has a great plan for your life, far greater than you could ever imagine.

Part of God's grace for me in the spring of 1984 was renewing my feeling of self-worth. I truly feel that the Lord brought Donna Greenough into my life to be part of this process.

I first met Donna on December 26, 1983, after I had moved out of my home into a friend's condominium in Laguna Beach. I was depresssed so I decided to go for a walk on the beach even though the sky was overcast and it was misting. Donna was the only other person on the beach.

Soon after I said hello to her, I told her that I was married and had two children. I didn't want to mislead her. I could tell that she was startled by my bluntness. I could also see that she was wondering, *If he has a family and is happily married, what's he doing here alone the day after Christmas?*

"My wife and I are separated," I said to answer her silent question. "She is going to file for a divorce in a few days."

"I'm going through a similar experience," she answered softly. "I've been separated from my husband for a year and a half. It looks as though he's going to file for divorce also."

As we talked that day and walked the beach together I felt I had met someone who understood the grief I felt. In the next weeks I met Donna several times for coffee and we shared our problems and comforted each other.

After we'd known each other for several months, I asked Donna, "Why did you put up with me during those early weeks?" I realized that in the beginning she had been a counselor and friend, not a girlfriend.

She answered my question quite truthfully. "I don't know why I put up with you. That's why I feel the Lord brought us together. If it had been up to me, I wouldn't have continued to see you. I had enough challenges of my own at that time." In addition to the divorce proceedings Donna had just been laid off by Continental Airlines because they were facing bankruptcy.

I know that our friendship helped me believe in myself again. This lovely young woman, who was extremely personable and intelligent, felt I was an interesting companion. We enjoyed several activities together, and we began exchanging books that interested us, like the *The Prophet* by Kahlil Gibran and *The Road Less Traveled* by Scott Peck. Donna and my family and friends helped me to regain my self-respect.

Don't Box Your God

The theme of Jampolsky's book, *Love Is Letting Go of Fear*, is that fear keeps us from being able to love. I believe that fear is the barrier that keeps us from feeling God's love. Some of us are afraid that in coming close enough to God to feel his love, we may find out that he isn't everything we thought he was. Perhaps our problems will not disappear as we think they should.

Other people fear that God will ask too much of them. After all, Jesus told the young lawyer to sell all he had and follow him. We want to follow God on our terms and we fear that we will lose this freedom. So we box God. We relegate him to Sunday mornings and shut him inside the church building.

The Hebrew people in the Old Testament tried to box God, just as we do. They began to believe that God lived in the Ark of the Covenant, and they put their trust in the ark rather than in the reality of a personal God who walked beside them in time of trouble.

They realized the error of their ways after a battle with their old adversaries, the Philistines. In the years before Israel was ruled by kings, the Philistines renewed their efforts to conquer the Holy Land. In one battle, four thousand Hebrew soldiers were killed before the Israelite army turned and fled.

Once they had regrouped, the Israelite leaders held a strategy meeting. "Why did God allow the Philistines to defeat us, his chosen people?" they asked each other. "For some reason, he is not with us," they decided.

It did not occur to them that God might be there, but they were the ones who were out of kilter. They had forgotten to ask for his help. They had forgotten to reach out to him in prayer. They had forgotten to follow his ways and had forsaken him for foreign gods.

"We'll make sure God's with us during the next battle," they decided. "Let's get the ark from Shiloh and carry it into battle with us."

Men carrying the Ark of the Covenant led the Israelite army into the next battle with the Philistines. But that battle was an even greater massacre than the first. Thirty thousand Hebrew soldiers died that day. And the Philistines carried away the Ark of the Covenant and set it up in the temple of their god, Dagon (where it caused so much sickness among the Philistines that they soon returned it to the Israelites).

One Hebrew woman was so horrified by the massacre that she named a baby born at this time "Ichabod," which means the glory has gone. And the Jews finally realized their God did not exist in a box called the Ark of the Covenant but was everywhere around them as they walked with him.

Don't box God as the Israelites did. He is not simply in church on Sunday morning. He's not in a particular place in our homes. He's not in a particular book. He is the light of the world. And where is light? Hidden in a corner somewhere? No, it is everywhere. It is all around you. It enfolds you.

Every step we take God is walking beside us. When we're driving down the freeway, he is with us. When we scold our children, he is with us. When we make mistakes at work, he is there. That's the promise of the verse, "I will fear no evil because you are with me."

How do we experience God's love? We must feel his love on a personal level as I did during that exercise with Gerald Jampolsky. We must pray the prayer, "Love me, Lord," and then we must reach out and take hold of God's love.

Reach Out to Him

God will not impose himself on you. He will not force you to love him. He has given us free will. We are not robots whom God controls from some computer high in the sky.

Instead we have to say, "Lord, I'll accept your love." If not, his love is like the water that comes into our homes. We see the pipes that lead into the house. In fact, we can look under the kitchen sink and see the plumbing, so we believe that water is available to us. But we can't use that water until we turn the faucet on and take it.

If you reach out to God, you will feel his love as I did that day with Gerald Jampolsky. The story of a prisoner who returned home expresses the tremendous feeling of love and forgiveness I felt after that exercise.

Having spent several years in jail, this man was finally released on parole. He wrote his wife to tell her the news and ended by saying, "Darling, I have embarrassed you terribly. I have been a disgrace to you and the family, and I will understand if you do not want me to come home. I will be on a train that arrives in our town at 3:00 P.M. on January 21.

"As the train comes into town I'll look to see if a

yellow ribbon is tied to the signpost. If it's there, I'll get off the train. If it isn't, I'll stay on the train and make a new life somewhere else. You'll never have to see me again."

I can imagine that man's apprehension as he came closer and closer to his hometown. Would the yellow ribbon be around the post? As the train pulled out of the town next to his and he began to see the familiar stores and landmarks of home, he must have been almost afraid to watch for the ribbon. What if his wife had not received the letter? What if she had forgotten the date of his arrival? What if his many mistakes had turned her love into hatred and she could not forgive him?

He must have squinted his eyes to see ahead. Finally, in the distance he could see something large and yellow wrapped around the signpost. A yellow sheet! Then he noticed that yellow seemed to be everywhere! Yellow pillowcases and shirts hung from the trees around the railroad station. His wife had tied every piece of yellow fabric she could find to any object that would hold a piece of cloth! Her love for her husband was that immense.

God's love for you is even greater. You might not feel that you deserve it. You might not know why he would love you so much, but he does. His arms are open wide. "I love you just the way you are," he says. "Come to me and I will give you rest."

O Lord,
give me
the self-esteem
to believe in me.

And a vision to see
where you want
this child to be.

STEP SEVEN

✣ ✣ ✣

Hold On to Hope.

"Your rod and Your staff, they comfort me."

There were times in my childhood when I was convinced that the only verse my parents knew was: "Spare the rod and spoil the child." Of course, during that same period, my parents thought that the only verse I knew in the Bible was: "Children will rise up against parents."[1]

What I'm saying is that I was a typical boy. I got into all the typical boyhood troubles. I played outside in my Sunday clothes when I wasn't supposed to; I teased my four sisters and got into scraps with them; I didn't clean up my room; my school grades weren't always good; and I snitched cookies from the cookie jar between meals.

Was I a juvenile delinquent? Of course not. I was spunky and curious and mischievous. My improper behavior at times was a part of growing up. I needed someone to correct my actions so I could learn right from wrong and so I could mature in judgment. My parents made sure I received that correction—and, believe me, sometimes it came in strong doses.

My folks had a discipline system very similar to the United States' courts of justice in that they felt the punishment should be given in accordance to the severity of the crime. Sometimes this meant I would only receive a scolding for what I had done wrong. Other times it meant I would get my hands slapped. But for something major, I could expect a spanking.

I dreaded spankings. My father has huge hands. They look so majestic when he raises them to pronounce a benediction on a congregation, but when those hands are used to give a couple of slaps across the backside you can take my word for it, they get the job done. My mother is thin and quite feminine, so she kept a wooden spoon handy so her spankings could make the impression they were supposed to make.

My parents loved me and my four sisters so much, they took the time to make sure we would grow up to respect authority, to love God, to appreciate other people, to obey rules, and to mind our manners. They never abused us, but they did not shirk using whatever discipline was needed in order to "train up a child in the way he should go."

As a youngster, my parents never said to me, "You are bad." Instead they said that what I had done was bad, that it was wrong and should not be done again. My parents combined love with discipline so I would understand that my behavior needed correcting, yet what I had done had not decreased their love for me.

Each time I was punished, I was also comforted. After I was scolded, my mom or dad would tousle my hair, smile at me, and say, "I still love you. It's okay, Robert. Go ahead and play now." If I had to have my hands slapped, my folks would give me a little hug and say, "You're a good boy. Just be more careful from now on, okay?" If I was given a spanking, I would be pulled up on Dad's or Mom's knee and hugged tenderly. I would be held and comforted until my tears stopped. They would pat my head and tell me they still loved me.

It was this combination of discipline and love, of justice and comforting, of correction and forgiveness that helped me grow up with a thorough understanding of correct behavior. As a child, I could not appreciate it the way I can today. I know now that I was truly blessed to have loving and wise parents.

God's Justice and Comforting

Have you ever stopped to think how tragic your life might have been if your parents had not disciplined you as a child? If your mother had not slapped your hands when you were two years old and told you not to play with the stove, today you might have scars from severe burns. If your father had not spanked you when you stole apples from the neighbor's tree, you might have advanced to more serious crimes until you wound up in prison.

There is a comfort in growing up with parents whom you can trust to keep you on the straight and narrow. When they discipline you and say, "This is for your own good," they really mean it.

God, our Heavenly Father, works the same way. Because he loves us, he parents us with both justice and comforting. David likened God to a shepherd who carried a rod and a staff. The rod was for punishment and justice, but the staff was for rescuing and comforting.

A shepherd's rod was very similar to a billy club or the nightstick carried these days by metropolitan police officers. It had a variety of uses. If a wild animal or a rustler tried to make off with one of the sheep, the shepherd could crack open the head of the invader with one swift blow. The rod could be used to spread the fleece of the animals so they could be inspected for cuts, bruises, parasites, infections, or dislocated bones. The rod also could be used to nudge and prod hesitant sheep to move back to the safety of the herd. The rod was a source of authority and power and protection.

A shepherd also carried a staff. This was a long, sturdy pole with a crook, or hook, on one end. If a sheep's wool got tangled in hillside brambles, the shepherd could reach his staff into the brush and hook it around the sheep and pull it free. Similarly, when an animal fell into a mud hole or became wedged between rocks, the staff could be used as a lift or wedge to free the animal. When a lamb was born, the shepherd could lift it with the staff and carry it to the mother; this kept the human scent off the newborn and helped the mother recognize the lamb as her own. The staff was in constant use by the shepherd to rescue sheep from dilemmas and to help them in times of need.

David saw the need for the Good Shepherd also to have a rod and a staff in order to be able to comfort his flock. God's rod is his sense of justice, the examining he does of our lives. God also has a staff of assistance to help us, namely Jesus. When we become entangled in the thorns of sin, God's staff responds to our prayers of need and pulls us free again. When we become wedged amidst the troubles of life, Jesus pries us loose and leads us back to the safety of his watch and care.

We may wonder at times why both the rod and the staff are needed. Why must we endure the disciplining and cleansing as part of the rescuing and comforting? Doesn't God love us enough just to take us the way we are?

Let me answer that question by drawing an analogy between God's love for us and your love for your children. Do you love your children at all times? I'm sure you do. Nevertheless, when your little ones come to the door and they are covered from head to toe in mud after an afternoon of making mud pies, do you quickly embrace them and hold them closely to you? Ugh!—no way!

When my children look like that, I grab an ear and hold them at arm's length and march them straight up to the bathtub. After they have bathed and lathered and had their hair washed, *then* (and only then) I bundle them up in a big towel and cuddle them close to me. We share little kisses and hugs, and I tell them how much daddy loves them.

I love my children even when they're dirty, just as you love your children whenever they get dirty. Still, as loving parents, we recognize the need for cleansing in order to draw us closer to the ones we love. Sin is a filth that separates us from God. The cleansing power of his rod enables us to be drawn closer to our Father.

Restoring Honor

After your children have been bathed and they're dressed in their clean pajamas and are sitting on your lap waiting for a bedtime story, does your mind continue to think of how dirty they were when they came in after playing? No, of course not. You've forgotten about all that. You've allowed your children to clean up and to restore their "honored" positions as the pride and joy of your family. You don't harp about their former unclean condition.

God forgives just as freely and allows us to retain our honored positions in his family. In fact, his forgiveness is even greater than ours, for he has the power actually to *forget* our sins.

This reminds me of the story of the woman who told people she could talk directly to Jesus. People came to her and she prayed with them. Soon, she had an effective ministry. About this time, she was approached by the bishop of her denomination, who had been watching her ministry with a great deal of skepticism.

"I understand that you claim to be able to talk to Jesus and that he talks back to you," said the bishop.

The woman nodded and replied, "Yes, that's true."

"If that's so, prove it," said the bishop. "The next time you talk to Jesus, ask him what I confessed to him in my last prayer."

A week later, the bishop happened to run into the woman at a church function. "Well, tell me," said the bishop, "did you talk to Jesus this week?"

"Yes, I did," said the woman.

"And did you ask him what my last confession was?"

"Yes."

"Well, what did Jesus tell you?"

The elderly woman shrugged her shoulders and replied, "Jesus said he forgot."

Isn't that wonderful? Jesus completely forgets the things we ask him to forgive. He restores our honor before him. Having restored our *honor*, we are then open to *opportunities* for service, positions of *leadership*, and the development of a personal *determination* to be successful.

This then leads us to our seventh step in getting through the going-through stage: Hold on to hope. I've devised an acrostic to help me remember the principles of holding onto hope. It goes like this: HOLD: *H*onor, *O*pportunity, *L*eadership, and the *D*etermination.

Recognizing Opportunities

As part of understanding the need to maintain our "honored" position in the family of God, I have included in this chapter a prayer which General Douglas MacArthur wrote regarding the honored position he desired for his son to hold both in his physical, earthly family and in his spiritual, heavenly family.

If we secure a righteous and noble honor, we are then able to view the world from a new perspective. From this perspective we can also see new opportunities open to us for service to God and our fellow man.

I like to be with people who are opportunity-minded. These people are usually optimistic, enthusiastic, and upbeat. They are the kind of people who look at an upset apple cart and say, "Wow! Neat! I've just discovered applesauce!" They are the kind of people who look at singed glass and say, "That's not ruined glass, that's the invention of sunglasses." Opportunity-minded people discover opportunities to advance because they are *looking* for opportunities.

In his book, *Staying Ahead of Time,* Dennis E. Hensley tells a story of how opportunity-minded Henry Ford always was. One day a businessman was being given a tour of the executive offices of the Ford Motor Company in Dearborn, Michigan. As the visitor passed one door, he saw a man seated at a desk with his feet propped up and his fingers laced behind his head. The man was doing nothing but daydreaming.

When the tour was over, the visitor asked Henry Ford who the man was who just sat at his desk relaxing.

"Oh, him?" said Ford. "That's Harkinson. He once had an idea that saved my company a million dollars in production costs. I'm keeping him on salary so that if he ever gets another idea, I'll have the opportunity to put it right into effect."

That little anecdote reminds us that people see opportunities from different perspectives. To the visitor in that story, the man who was relaxing was a daydreamer. To

Henry Ford, that man was a thinker.

Perspective is so important. In front of the main house at Rancho Capistrano, sitting high on a hill overlooking the highway below, is a lovely fieldstone patio with wrought-iron tables and chairs. To keep the outdoor furniture dust free, we cover the chairs with white plastic garbage bags. One windy day, the plastic bags were blown sideways on the chairs. They formed peaks on one corner. A person who drove by on Interstate 5, the major highway that crosses the valley, glanced our way and saw many pointed white shapes. He called the police and reported, "A Ku Klux Klan rally is being held at Rancho Capistrano!"

Believe it or not, the police drove out to investigate the charge. When they saw the pointed white garbage bags, we all shared a big laugh. It reminded me, though, that perspective makes all the difference in assessing a situation.

If your perspective of yourself is that you are a worthless individual, you will not find opportunities before you. But, if you see yourself as a child of God and as an honored member of his family, you'll find a limitless number of opportunities open to you. To make use of these opportunities, you must be willing to accept a role of leadership.

Accepting Leadership

To me, the roughest part of being a leader is making command decisions that will have an effect on other people. I remember one such situation early in my ministry.

While the remodeling work was being done on John Crean's old warehouse, the members of our congregation needed a place to meet. The only available spot was at the foot of the hill where there was a large cleared area that John used as parking lot. I stood on the hillside and the congregation sat in chairs at the foot of the hill. The only problem was in spring and summer. That year San Juan Capistrano had a rainy season equal to no other.

We were always afraid that if we set up the chairs and sound equipment outdoors, the odds were that it would rain on us.

I prayed about this dilemma and then told Nate Morrison and his crew of workers to step up everything at 8:00 each Sunday. One Sunday morning I received a call from Nate at exactly 8:00.

"What should we do, pastor? We're out here ready to set up chairs for the 9:30 A.M. service, but it's pouring."

I hesitated a moment. "But it isn't raining here, Nate."

"Well, you should see it here! You'll get it soon."

"Wait a while to see if the rain lets up. Set up by 8:30 regardless of whether it's raining or not."

"In the rain?"

"That's right. We'll pray that God will stop the rain in time for the service."

Forty-five minutes later Nate called back. "The rain has stopped, Robert. Everything is ready for the 9:30 service. I'm glad you told us to go ahead."

For the next fourteen Sundays it rained all around our district, but not one drop fell on our property during the services. It was a year of record water damage. Bridges washed out, beaches washed away, and roads were destroyed. But we never missed a service. We did what was right and we acted on faith. God honored the leadership role that I took for our congregation and that our church took for the community.

Effective leadership is usually derived from an internal determination to succeed. Without determination, a leader cannot be the driving force that is required for group success.

Forming Determination

When you stop to consider it, determination has been the factor that has made the difference in the success or failure of most well-known individuals. Without determination, Helen Keller would have yielded to her deafness and blindness and never learned to read and write. Without determination, Franklin Roosevelt would have yielded to polio and never become president. Without determination, Jack London would have yielded to poverty and not become the first author in the world to earn a million dollars from writing.

Let me tell you the story of Colleen Johnson, the lovely black woman who is my mother's executive secretary and who has been part of the Crystal Cathedral ministry for almost twenty years. Colleen was born and raised in Philadelphia. When she was seventeen she married Ed Carter, a young electrician.

Three years later, her husband encouraged Colleen to retire and become a full-time housewife. Their little girl was two years old and he wanted his wife to be at home with her. Ten days later, at the age of twenty-five, Ed died of cerebral paralysis. Soon after her husband's death, Colleen realized she was pregnant.

"I turned to my brother for help," Colleen says. "He was two years older than I was and at seminary. About nine months later he had a heart attack and died. More than ever before I realized that the Lord is the only one I can hold on to."

Eight years later, Colleen married again. "I was looking for someone who had about the same temperament I did, someone who was a Christian, someone who loved children, and someone who wanted to come to California, as I did." Colleen always laughs as she adds her final prerequisite.

And that's what she and her new husband, Jimmy Johnson, did. About a year after they arrived in Orange County, they began to attend my dad's drive-in church.

Jimmy and Colleen had two sons, Mark, their older, and Glenn, a special child who was born with many abnormalities. Immediately after his birth, he had surgery to construct a rectal opening, which had not formed in utero. Later the doctors discovered that Glenn was mentally retarded.

Glenn attended the Kenneth Mitchell School in Santa Ana for trainable retarded children. When he was only four years old he was selected as the school's May Day King to reign with a queen who was twenty-one years old. Everyone who knew Glenn loved him for his enthusiastic spirit and abundant love. Glenn died at the age of fourteen.

Still Colleen held on to hope. She held on to her faith in God and determined to live up to her honored position as his child. Even Glenn's death could be an opportunity, and the courageous way Colleen kept up with her work in the church witnessed to God's ability to comfort her in times of trouble. His death also became an opportunity for others to remember him in a way that would benefit his handicapped brothers and sisters.

Since Glenn had just been learning to ride a bicycle, the Kiwanis Club and other people got together and donated money for a Glenn Johnson Memorial Bike Trail, which is used also by the Orange County Special Olympics. Now other boys and girls at the school have a sheltered bike trail on which to practice their bike-riding skills before they tackle the distractions of riding in their own neighborhoods.

In 1977, Jimmy Johnson, Colleen's second husband, became ill with cancer. He went through two surgeries and the cancer seemed to go into remission. But in 1979 cancer appeared in his liver, and he died just before Christmas of that year.

During all of these years, I never saw Colleen without a smile on her face. She was always an encouragement to our family. Once I asked Colleen how she managed to keep such a positive attitude despite all that had happened to her.

"I have someone I can hold on to. I always have had and I always will, no matter what happens. I will always smile because he loves and cares for me."

If you've had some tough times, maybe lost a husband, maybe like Colleen you've lost two, maybe on top of that your favorite brother and even a teenage child, you need the same Person to hold on to. He's willing to help if you just reach out to him. When you do, He will give you the determination to overcome your difficulties.

Robert A. Schuller

God Always Answers

We have seen how our prayer of "Hold me, Lord" can be enhanced by the four elements of HOLD: *H*onor, *O*pportunities, *L*eadership, and *D*etermination. Before we leave this topic, let's now take a moment to consider the ways God may elect to respond to our prayers. Personally, I believe God answers all prayers, but often his response is so different from what we are expecting that we can begin to think he hasn't heard us.

It is not my purpose here to engage in long dissertations on theological views of prayer. Instead, let me just say God usually gives one of four responses to our prayers. He will tell us *no, grow, slow,* or *go.*

When the Answer is No

When God says no to us, we can be assured that he has a reason. Sometimes the things we pray for are not right, or at least not right for us as individuals. What may be right for me may not be part of God's plan for you, and vice versa.

Sometimes God may say no because the timing is wrong. I had wanted to hold services in the Mission Drive-in Theater: God said, "No!" It was the best thing that ever happened. I still got good publicity, but I didn't have any traffic problems with the eventual site at Saddleback Community College.

Once, when I was leading a group of travelers on a tour of the Holy Land, a man named Dr. Anderson was in my group. The doctor was confined to a wheelchair as the result of an injury he sustained in the Second World War. This man had always wanted to tour Israel but had never found time for it. Now, he was very ill, and he decided to make the trip. He told me that he had prayed and begged God to let him live long enough to tour the Holy Land.

The flight to the Middle East was long and strenuous, and I could tell that it had exhausted Dr. Anderson. Nevertheless, at our first stop in Amman, Jordan, he insisted on spending the whole day sight-seeing with the rest of our group. And all that day Dr. Anderson could only talk about how excited he was because the next day we would be going to Israel.

But Dr. Anderson never made it to Israel. He was so weak that night he had to be taken to the hospital. He died only a few days later. I never have understood why God denied this man his prayerful desire to see Israel. Yet, God said no to Dr. Anderson. God heard the prayer but chose not to fulfill it.

Moses prayed to be allowed to enter the Promised Land. God answered, "No." David prayed to be allowed to build God's holy temple. God answered, "No." Jesus prayed to have the crucifixion pass from him. God answered, "No." All Christians must come to grips with the fact that God answers all prayers, but sometimes his answer is, "No." That's not easy to accept, but it is a reality.

Grow

Sometimes God instructs us to grow, and then he will fulfill our prayer requests. When I was seventeen and out of high school, I announced that I was going into full-time ministry work. My parents told me I was still a minor and until I was eighteen I would do what they told me to. And that meant going to college.

I prayed to God, asking for a chance to enter the ministry as soon as I turned eighteen. Instead I was sent to college. Once I arrived and began to attend classes, I realized how shallow my preparation for the ministry was. I couldn't read Greek or Hebrew. I had no knowledge of Old Testament history and geography and philosophy. In fact, I didn't even know how to study properly.

God was gracious to me. He answered my prayer with the word *grow.* I spent the next several years in a liberal arts college and seminary and then at work at the Crystal Cathedral. After all this maturing and growing, God answered my original prayer and gave me a ministry.

Later when I asked God to give me John Crean's property for my church, God again said, "Grow!" He made me first get my church organized and my ministry established. Two years later, when I was ready, God answered my prayer.

Slow

At times, God's response to our prayers is for us to proceed slowly. Some things in life must be done at a pace that allows one to truly comprehend and appreciate what is transpiring.

Could you glance at a painting by Rembrandt for ten seconds and fully appreciate it? No. You need to stare at it for a long time in order to determine the blend of paint colors, the movement of brush strokes, the focus of the lighting, and the balance of the image on the canvas.

Could you listen just once to a symphony by Beethoven and fully appreciate it? No. You need to hear it many times in order to pick out the harmonies, distinguish the various instruments, recognize the different rhythms, and study the distinct movements. If you think of your favorite symphonies or popular songs, you will realize that they are all melodies you have heard many times, often so frequently that you whistle or hum the tune without even thinking.

God wants us to slow down at times. He wants to teach us appreciation for what we have. When I began my church, I prayed for an attendance of two hundred. Instead, I had only fifty. But when that doubled to one hundred and then doubled again to two hundred, I had a much better knowledge of who the members of my church were. God had given me time to learn their names and talents. In that way, everyone was given a responsibility. No one was a number. Everyone was an individual. God's plan taught me patience and planning. He was right in telling me to go slowly.

If God is showing you how to enjoy and savor life, don't try to rush ahead of him. He knows what is best for you.

Go

Naturally, the most exciting response to prayer that God can give us is a clear command to "Go!" Often God will respond this way. He told Moses to go before Pharaoh. He told Joshua to go forth and conquer the Promised Land. He told David to go to battle to reclaim the Jewish territories.

Occasionally, people come to me and say, "Pastor, I'm scared. I want to start this new business (new job or new school), and I've prayed to God for guidance but I'm still hesitant to act. You tell me what I should do."

Donna and I faced such a major decision in the fall of 1984. My relationship with her had grown into a very deep and sincere love. The feeling was mutual. After a great deal of prayer, we decided that God had healed each of us and generated such a warm friendship between us that he was leading us into marriage.

We went to a dear friend, Dr. Herman Ridder. He had been my counselor throughout my going-through stage. We were worried. Were we making a rational decision? Was God telling us, "Go!"?

Dr. Ridder, my family, Donna, and I all felt that the answer was yes. We announced our plans to the congregation to be married on November 10. Everyone attended. Again I felt their loving support. Roger Williams played the piano. Tom Tipton sang, and my father and Dr. Ridder performed the ceremony.

I'm convinced that when God says, "Go!" we have to be ready to go. Many people respond to his call when all odds seem to be against them, people like Patty Wilson, a young woman who has epilepsy.

Patty had had a few convulsions as a preschooler. Then one day when Patty was seven, she had a severe attack in school and she began to shake so hard that she fell to the floor. Her eyes rolled back in her head. The next day the other children avoided her. Over the years Patty's attacks increased, and the doctors finally diagnosed her problem as epilepsy.

But God told Patty to go despite her handicap. When

Patty was fifteen years old, she decided to run from Los Angeles to Portland, Oregon, to prove to others that epileptics are normal people and to raise funds for the National Epilepsy Foundation.

By the end of the first day of her marathon, her foot was aching so badly she could hardly stand on it. But Patty would not stop. The pain grew progressively worse in the next few days. Finally Patty's parents convinced her to see a doctor.

"You have a stress fracture," the doctor said after examining her foot carefully. "You must stop the marathon so it can heal."

"But, doctor, I've got to complete the race," she replied immediately.

"Patty, that's impossible! I've got to set the fracture."

"Well, what would happen if you set the fracture in a few weeks, when I'm done with the run?" Patty suggested. "I've made a commitment. I have to fulfill it."

"But, Patty, if I bind it so you can run, you will get blisters."

"What are a few blisters? . . . Nothing more than water under the skin. My mother could take a syringe and let out the water and I could keep going."

And that's just what Patty did. The doctor showed her parents how to wrap her foot tightly with tape. Each day Patty ran twenty-five to thirty miles, despite the pain in her foot, despite two epileptic seizures. Patty ran for forty-two more days.

When she finally got within a mile of the city of Portland, the mayor joined her. Together they ran into the city and under a banner which read: "Run, Patty. Run." Patty Wilson ran 1,310 miles on a fractured foot.

When God says go, he will hold you. Just hold on to hope and he will get you to the finish line, just as he did Patty.

General Douglas MacArthur's Prayer for His Child

Lord, build me a son who'll be strong enough to know when he is weak and brave enough to face himself when he is afraid. One who will be proud and unbending in honor and humble and gentle in victory.

Build me a son, Lord, whose wishes will not take the place of deeds; a son who will know thee, and that to know himself is a foundation stone of knowledge. Lead him I pray not in the path of ease and comfort but under the stress and spurs of difficulties and challenge. Here let him learn to stand up in the storm. Here let him learn compassion for those who fail.

Build me a son, O Lord, whose heart will be clear, whose goal will be high; a son who will master himself before he seeks to master other men. One who will reach into the future, yet never forget the past.

And after all these things are his, add, I pray, a sense of humor so that he may always be serious yet never take himself too seriously. Give him humility so that he may always remember the simplicity of true greatness, the open mind of true wisdom, and the meekness of true strength. Then I, his father, will dare to whisper I have not lived in vain.

God
often stretches us
to the breaking point
before stepping in.

STEP EIGHT

✣ ✣ ✣

Believe It, You Can Do It!

"You prepare a table before me in the presence of my enemies."

A member of my congregation, Ben Ward, served as a pilot in the U.S. Armed Services from 1938 to 1959. During World War II Ben had a job that literally took him into the presence of his enemies week after week.

"I was a glider pilot in Europe," recalls Ben. "I flew the big CG-4A gliders that could transport fourteen troopers. A tow plane would take off from England, France, or Italy, pulling me into the combat zones over Germany and Holland. We then would cut loose and land as best we could."

Ben's aircraft landed in mine fields, next to machine gun nests, in barbed-wire fences, and nosed into trenches. "We didn't call them landings," Ben says. "We referred to them as controlled crashes. Once I got the thing down, I had to leave it and try to make my way to friendly forces so I could get back to my base for another flight."

According to Ben, the glider was so big and unwieldy, it took all his concentration to control it. "People have asked me if I felt scared during those flights, but the truth is, I was so busy trying to keep the glider steady and on target, I didn't have time to worry.

"A glider pilot did all his worrying the night before his flight. I used to lie in my bunk and think about all that could go wrong. And there was plenty—a tow line could break, a wind current could imbalance us, a landing could be fatal. The glider had no motors for control and no metal for protection. It was big, slow, and vulnerable.

"You can never really appreciate the lonely terror of being in the presence of your enemies until it really happens to you," Ben says. "I can remember scrambling from my glider and trying to find a hiding place before the Nazis would start shelling the aircraft. It often was every man for himself. I would crawl on my stomach and keep low, hoping the bursting flares would not enable a sniper to see me and pick me off. Sometimes I would bury my head in my arms and just try to rest. I knew that if I was discovered, I would be killed.

"I've been asked where I got the courage to fly all those missions. My answer is that I always felt I had a Helping Hand guiding me in each of those flights. I flew gliders during the whole war, and I never sustained any serious injury. That experience strengthened my understanding of how God can protect me even in the presence of my enemies.

"My wife, Inez, is a fine Christian woman, and I have drawn closer to God through her strong testimony. She believes that God responded to her prayers for my protection during the war. I believe that, too. God really does care for his children."

Our eighth step in getting through the going-through stage is: believe it, you can do it. Your trust in God should outweigh your fear of your enemies. The Bible tells us that through God we are "more than conquerors."

In the Presence of Your Enemies

David knew God wanted him to develop a greater trust of God's protection of him, so he wrote, "You prepare a table before me in the presence of my enemies."

This sounds almost bizarre, doesn't it? To be logical, it seems as though it should say, "You prepare a battleground . . . a boxing arena . . . an assault field . . . or a combat zone in the presence of my enemies." Yet, that's not what David said. He said God would prepare a table where David could dine and talk with his enemies. How strange!

As a child, I was confused by this verse. I pictured in my mind a nice picnic table covered with plates of fried chicken, baked potatoes, tossed salad, and all my favorite foods; sitting around this table, however, were all the bullies and roughnecks from my school. In order to enjoy the food, I would have to sit amid my enemies.

The very thought of it sent chills up and down my backbone.

As I got older, I embellished my mental interpretations of that verse. I imagined myself as a soldier fighting a trench war. As I lay huddled in my trench, I heard our general call out my name. When I peeked over the top, I could see him out in the middle of no man's land between our trench and the enemy's. He was standing beside a pretty table set with lots of food. The general kept calling to me and telling me to join him for a meal. All I could think of was, "Go out there? Are you crazy? No way! We'd be eating right in plain sight of the enemy."

God is not hesitant to place us in the midst of our enemies. The Bible contains numerous accounts of how God brought his spokesmen before their enemies in order that his power and strength would be made evident. Moses was led before Pharaoh. Daniel was led before Nebuchadnezzar. Christ was led before Pilate. In each instance, God used the circumstances to assert his authority as Lord and Master.

Confronting one's enemies can be a very enlightening experience. Often, what we fear most is more imaginary than real. The Wizard of Oz seemed terrifying to Dorothy and her companions until the little dog Toto pulled back the curtain and revealed the wizard to be a small man who used a machine to make himself appear greater than he was. Life is often like that. We frequently discover that our enemies are nowhere near as fierce as we imagined them to be.

With God on our side, *we* become the ones whom others tremble over. The Bible says, "If God is for us, who can be against us?"[2]

Face Your Fears

In the depths of the Great Depression, President Franklin Roosevelt told the American public, "We have nothing to fear but fear itself." F.D.R. knew that an unbridled imagination can lead to fear, then panic, and finally hysteria. He wanted the people to realize that if they faced their problems squarely and didn't believe the propaganda of the enemies, they would be reminded that America was strong, powerful, and self-sufficient.

How about you? Have you ever faced your enemies as Ben Ward has? Have you ever asked yourself who your enemies are, why they became your enemies, how they view you, and in what ways you are alike and in what ways different? It can be a startling exercise.

In Erich Maria Remarque's classic novel about World War I, *All Quiet on the Western Front*, there is a poignant scene in which a young German soldier is pinned down in a foxhole with the body of a French soldier he has killed in hand-to-hand combat. The young soldier begins to talk to the corpse. He apologizes for killing the man, cries over the grief he has caused the man's family, and laments the fact that they didn't meet under different circumstances and become friends. What causes this terrible feeling of guilt and shock is the fact that the two men are so alike—same age, same build, same military rank. It all emphasizes to the German soldier how futile and foolish war is. If we are all so alike, why do we become enemies of one another, he wonders.

Are you and *your* enemies so vastly different that you couldn't even sit down to dinner together? Have you ever looked across that table and found yourself looking into a mirror and discovering that you were your own worst enemy? That can happen, you know. Any time you doubt your capabilities or downplay your accomplishments or show indifference to your potential, you become your own worst enemy.

Why should we be afraid of any thing or any person? God protects us even in the worst of situations. He was with Moses at the Red Sea. He was with Daniel in the lion's den. He was with David during the duel against Goliath. He was with Paul and Silas in prison. He's always there to watch over us and to put a protective arm around us.

Confidence Amid Tragedy

God takes care of us. He does it his own way, and although we may not recognize it as a blessing, it is. Let me explain by telling you again about my sister Carol.

I told you in an earlier chapter that Carol is an expert skier despite the fact she has only one leg. After the accident that took Carol's leg, she was hospitalized for more than 270 days. She missed an entire year of school, of church, of sports, of virtually everything.

To say that Carol was seriously hurt in the accident is a tremendous understatement. She lost twenty-three pints of blood. The human body only contains thirteen pints of blood. She was losing blood faster than the doctors could get it back into her body intravenously. When the paramedics pulled Carol's body from the ditch where the crash occurred, they could not feel a pulse. Even in the emergency room her pulse could only be detected by machine. She was weak and on the verge of death.

For months on end Carol fought for her life. She suffered from internal injuries, recurring infections, and the emotional and physical pain of a leg amputation. You might wonder, *Where was God when Carol needed him? Why didn't God save Carol from that accident?* Perhaps a better question would be, why did God spare Carol's life and allow her to go on with her life? Carol herself has the best answer to that.

I'll never forget my sister's behavior the first time I went to see her at Children's Hospital of Orange County. I was nervous about seeing Carol. I didn't know how to soothe her or what to say. Here she was literally torn limb from limb and I was supposed to be a comforting brother and minister, able to cheer her up. Yet, I didn't know what to say.

I entered Carol's hospital room and found her propped up in bed and smiling. Before I could say anything, Carol announced, "Bob, I know that God has great things in store for my life. I am going to be able to minister to people who normally wouldn't pay attention to me. God is using me for something great. He's preparing me for something special."

Carol was right about that. She has appeared on television to give her testimony; she has been written about in books and magazines and has written her own book, *In the Shadow of His Wings*; and, as I noted before, she has become a champion skier. She has inspired thousands of people to live positive lives.

As my sister proved, "All things work together for good to those who love God, to those who are called according to His purpose."[3] Yes, God does protect us and care for us in the presence of our enemies, whether the enemies are persons or tragic circumstances.

Having Abundant Lives

The metaphor of Christ as the Good Shepherd in Psalm 23 reminds me of how diligently a real shepherd works to offer abundant care for his sheep. Shepherds move their flocks into the tablelands and low mountains each summer. The air is cooler there, and the fresh, lush spring grass on the mountain plateaus is plentiful. Prior to moving the flocks, the shepherd scouts the areas carefully in order to locate the finest meadow. He locates a spot with adequate water. He builds lean-tos and sheds to protect the sheep from storms. He puts out salt licks and fresh straw to enhance the grazing areas. He fences off any dangerous cliffs and he fills in any pits or ditches. In short, he does everything possible to ensure the sheep will not want for anything.

God does not sponsor failures. He gives us everything we need to enjoy life. Those of us who live in America have had an extra portion of God's overflowing abundance. Why, then, do we sometimes feel as if we have been "slighted" or "cheated"?

In comparison to the vast majority of people on this planet, we live like kings. The United States has only 7.2 percent of the world's population, yet it owns 55 percent of all the money in the world. The average American eats four times as much food as his body requires. We live in opulence. To the average person in China or Russia or Central America who looks at our standard of living, we are wealthy beyond all comprehension.

I was reminded of this during my most recent visit to China. Even though the city of Peking had been modernized—it was quite common to see neon signs flashing advertisements for Coca-Cola and Sanyo and other brand-name products—people still rode bicycles. The average person in China may never even get a chance to ride in an automobile, much less own one.

Because automobiles are so astronomically expensive in China, one enterprising man had somehow managed to purchase one of the locally made automobiles and had set it in the center of the Forbidden City so people could pose beside it. He had a large old-fashioned camera mounted on a tripod and for a set amount of money the visitors to the city could sit in his car and have their pictures taken. The man was running a thriving business. How strange this seemed when compared to America where children start driving at age sixteen and most families own one or two cars!

Beyond all our material wealth, we Christians also have spiritual wealth—inward contentment, a sense of purpose, security, and peace of mind. These treasures are just another form of the abundance we receive from our Protector, the Good Shepherd. He delights in caring for us in every facet of our lives.

God's Protective Hand

If a stray lamb wanders from the flock and far away from the shepherd, it is vulnerable to attacks from mountain lions, wolves, and coyotes. It can easily be hurt or killed. If it stays close to the shepherd, it has continual protection. God works the same way. For greater protection, we need only draw nearer to him.

God has a wonderful plan for each of us. To help us

succeed at our goals in life, God has established laws of nature and laws of the spirit. As long as we work within these laws, we advance steadily toward our goals. These laws were created as part of God's protection for us. If we elect to go against them, we invite disaster.

In mentioning this, I'm reminded of an incident that happened at my father's church in Garden Grove, California, around 1970. Just shortly after the church had finished building the thirteen-story Tower of Hope, a mentally unstable man went to the roof of the structure and threatened to jump. When the authorities arrived, we were told the man had escaped that day from the psychological disorders ward of the University of California Irvine Medical Center and had purchased some illegal narcotics on the street. He now thought that he could fly, and he was determined to prove it by leaping off the Tower of Hope.

Although people tried to talk the man off the roof, he paid no heed. Instead he actually jumped from the building. Incredible as it may seem, he landed in the decorative pool of water, which is less than a foot deep, in the garden below and survived the fall with only a broken leg and some cuts and bruises. After hitting the water, he actually sat up, then stood, and soon hobbled away. Everyone was dumbfounded. It was incredible.

Why God chose to intervene and spare that man's life is a mystery to me. I can tell you this, however. Now that the man is well once more, he would never think of jumping off that tower again. His broken leg and bruised body gave him emphatic reminders that God will not alter the laws of nature just to please some individual's distorted view of what personal freedom should be.

In the same way, we cannot expect God to alter his spiritual laws for us. If we stray from the Good Shepherd, we must not be surprised by the injuries we may suffer as a natural consequence of our folly.

Earlier I spoke of glider pilot Ben Ward. Ben's greatest risks were faced on D-Day when he had to fly a glider into Normandy not once, not twice, but *three* times.

"My job was to take thirty infantrymen to the front on

the morning after D-Day in a British RAF Horse glider," recalls Ben. "We came in low and fast so as not to be discovered. The glider struck a row of thick hedges and jolted us so hard one of the soldiers broke his neck and was killed. The troops stayed, but I made my way back to the air base. I breathed more easily, thinking my part of the invasion was over.

"The next day the Nazis put up a greater resistance than anyone had expected. Our men got pinned down and needed more ammunition. I was ordered to take a glider with a full load of ammunition to the front. I couldn't believe it! One well-placed shot into my fuselage and I would be a giant Roman candle. This was really tempting fate, I felt. But I followed orders.

"Somehow, I managed to land the glider and get the crates of shells and bullets to the troops. I returned to the base and sat down exhausted. I had beaten death twice.

"Before I could head for the showers, I was summoned to the commander's office. He said that the engineers needed to start clearing a path for the jeeps and trucks to travel over. They needed me to get a small bulldozer into a glider and to deliver it to Normandy. This was incredible! To survive two flights was miraculous, but to go a third time was sheer insanity.

"I was dog-tired, tense, and apprehensive. Yet, as bad as I had it, I knew my cohorts on the beaches were having it just as bad, or worse. I took a deep breath and went to work. The flight was rugged because the fighting was at its peak. I put the glider down, delivered the bulldozer and four more soldiers, and then headed back. What a day. What a miracle!"

Ben knows from firsthand experience how God's protective hand can be upon people. So, too, does another man, whose name is very familiar: Mickey Rooney.

About ten years ago this popular actor saw my father on television. Mickey was feeling depressed and his career was at a low ebb. My father contacted him and helped him revitalize the Christianity that had been a part of his youth.

Today Mickey's testimony of faith is truly inspiring. "People think that famous people never have any worries. Let me tell you, they're wrong. I am famous, but that hasn't kept me from being ill. I am famous, but that hasn't prevented me from being broken-hearted. I am famous, but that hasn't stopped me from being dissatisfied with myself."

He adds, "But the most satisfying moment in my life was when I realized I was famous to the one person who really counts—Jesus Christ. When I accepted his love, I became a strong and faith-filled person."

Mickey's life changed miraculously after he reactivated his faith. He landed a lead role in the smash Broadway play, *Sugar Babies*; he was nominated for an Academy Award for his performance in *The Black Stallion*; and he was nominated for an Emmy Award for his TV performance in "Bill."

Sometimes our enemies can be other people, as was the case with glider pilot, Ben Ward. Sometimes our enemies can be the moods of depression and fear we face and must overcome as Mickey Rooney did. Through it all, God shows us how to face our enemies with triumphant confidence. Our faith leads us to victory every time.

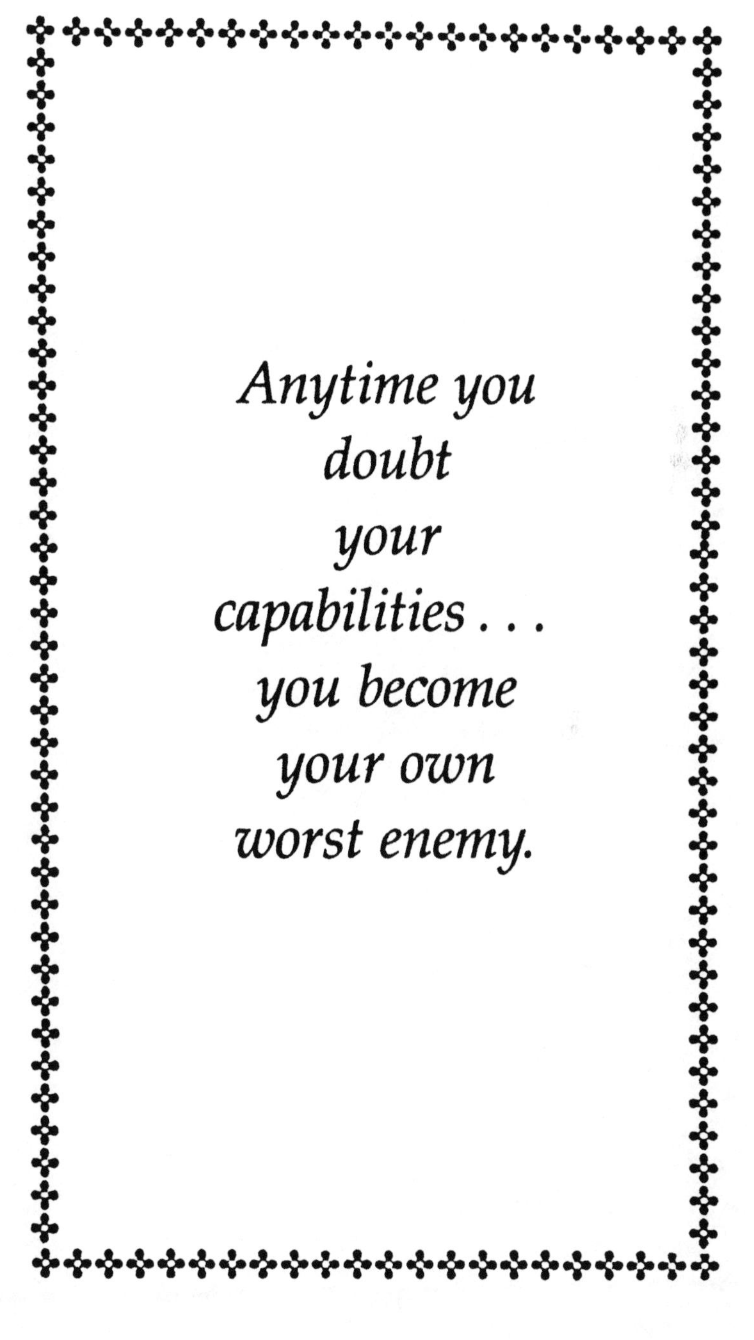

Anytime you
doubt
your
capabilities . . .
. . . you become
your own
worst enemy.

STEP NINE

✣ ✣ ✣

Your Future Will Be Fruitful.

"You anoint my head with oil. My cup runs over."

When most people pray a prayer such as, "Heal me, Lord," they are asking to be healed physically. To me, there's far more to being a healthy individual than simply having a physically fit body. Health, I believe, involves three different parts of our being: body, mind, and soul. Each part impacts upon the other. We will never really be physically healthy if our minds and souls are not healthy.

We need to learn how to relax and allow God to heal us from within. Verse five of the Twenty-third Psalm—"You anoint my head with oil"—speaks about healing as no other verse in the Bible does.

Physical Health

As a young boy, this verse confused me. Why on earth would I want somebody to be pouring salad oil all over my head? That gooey, rather slimy stuff? But once I studied the use of oil in biblical times the meaning became clear.

You see, olive oil was one of the main ointments for soothing a wound. If a lamb was injured and had an open cut, a good shepherd immediately poured oil on the wound.

The first promise God makes us in this verse is that he will heal our bodies. I believe God can heal us today, just as totally as Jesus and his disciples healed the sick in biblical times.

I know of quite a few modern-day miracles. Let me tell one, the story of Lory Jones, the wife of actor Dean Jones, who played in many Walt Disney films, such as *The Love Bug* and *The Shaggy D.A.*, and in television's "The Teddy Bears."

In February of 1974 Lory and Dean took a vacation to

Mexico City. One day when they were sightseeing they decided to tour a Catholic cathedral. As they followed the tour guide, Dean began making offhand comments like, "This place must be impossible to heat!" To Dean, the cathedral was just another architectural site. He was not prepared for the priest's final remark at the end of the tour.

"If some of you need physical healing," the priest said, "now is the time to pray."

Nor was he prepared for his wife's response to the priest's suggestion. Lory turned to Dean and said, "Let's pray for my arthritis." She was taking about thirty aspirins a day to relieve the pain in her hands. That morning Dean had massaged her hands to alleviate the cramping and pain so she could go sightseeing.

Dean almost laughed; only the thought of Lory's intense pain made him consider her suggestion seriously. *What have I got to lose?* he asked himself.

"A man of great faith, I wasn't," Dean admits. "But I couldn't resist my wife's request."

Dean bowed his head. He prayed silently. *God, heal Lory's arthritis.* Lory's prayer was much longer than that; however, within five minutes they were walking out of the cathedral.

"I think something happened in there," Lory said as they walked away from the cathedral.

"Great!" Dean answered as he thought, *If praying makes you feel better, that's fine.*

Three days later, Lory stopped taking aspirin. Dean watched her move her hands without wincing with pain. Surely this was a miracle. But would it last? They waited for the pain to return. Two weeks passed. A month. A year. Lory had truly been healed.

An Ounce of Prevention

Some people are healed dramatically as Lory Jones was, but the best kind of medicine is preventive medicine. As the saying goes, "An ounce of prevention is worth a pound of cure."

In March of 1984, my dad took my brothers-in-law and me to Cabo San Lucas at the very tip of the Baja Peninsula in Mexico. I was enjoying the warmth of a sunny day on the beach so much, I forgot to apply suntan oil until it was too late. By midafternoon I began to feel hot and look red. I learned a great deal about preventive medicine during the vacation, just as anyone does who sits out too long in the extremely hot Mexican sun.

A few days later I was teasing my dad about his refusal to drink any of the water. "After all, Dad, the water in the cape is okay. In fact, it's probably better than the water you drink in Los Angeles. Ninety-seven percent of the flu that tourists claim they get when they visit here is psychosomatic."

Dad replied, "Well, Robert, it's not the 97 percent I'm worried about. It's the 3 percent." Preventive medicine is without doubt the best medicine, and it is one of the blessings God is offering us in Psalm 23:5.

Oil was also used in biblical times as preventive medicine. In the summertime sheep were irritated by flies, particularly nose flies. The insects landed on a sheep's nose and laid their larvae inside its nostrils. The flies were so irritating to the sheep that the animal could not rest peacefully. Instead it was constantly stamping its legs and shaking its head to rid itself of the pests. A good shepherd solved this problem by anointing the sheep's head with oil so the flies could not land on it; he used preventive medicine.

If God is our Shepherd, he anoints your head with oil as you come to church every Sunday to worship him and fellowship with other Christians. He anoints your head with oil when you read the Bible. He anoints you when you come to him in prayer.

Some people say to me, "Why do I have to come to church on Sunday? I listen to the television preachers. That's my church for the week."

As the son of a well-known television minister, I'm extremely sensitive to the tendency some people have to allow the television ministry to replace the local church. Instead, this ministry should be a stepping stone. My father does not want his program to replace the local Sunday church service. A local church is often mentioned at the end of "The Hour of Power" to refer listeners to services in their own communities.

I believe we have to go to church and fellowship with other Christians in order to receive God's anointing. This preventive medicine keeps our minds and souls on track. Every day we must determine to let God's spirit and love direct our actions. It's a deliberate choice.

The songs on Debbie Boone's record album, *Choose Life*, express her decision to let God direct her actions. "I began to realize that God gives us choices in our lifetime. I decided I didn't want to make any more choices against his will or for myself. Since I have a choice, I decided to choose his will for me and his purpose for my life. I decided to choose life."

Does that cause problems for Debbie? Of course it does. Every day she has to make choices that may not seem good for her career according to Hollywood's perspective. For instance, she refuses to sing certain songs, which she knows will become popular, because of their suggestive lyrics. But she has decided to listen to God's voice rather than those that tell her what to do in order to enhance her career.

"I don't want a career if Jesus can't use me," she says. "He's my manager. Every morning I come before him and ask, 'What do you want from me today? What's the best I can do for you?' That's not easy," Debbie admits, "but it's always worth it."

When we're asking for God's guidance every day in prayer, as Debbie is, when we're attending church faithfully, when we're reading the Scriptures, our minds are protected from temptation by God's anointing. We are taking spiritual vitamins.

Mental Health

The second promise of the verse, "You anoint my head with oil," is that God will heal our minds. One Lenten season I asked my congregation to fast mentally rather than physically. "Let's fast against negative thinking," I suggested. "Let's see the word *Lent* as an acrostic: *L* et's *E* liminate *N* egative *T* hinking. During these forty days let's give up negative thinking and allow the oil of God to soothe us."

When we eliminate negative thinking, we strike at the core of many illnesses that affect the human body. Scientific studies are proving that our state of mind has a profound effect on the state of our health—for worse or for better. Our negative attitudes can made us disease-prone. Our positive attitudes can make us health-prone.

Dr. Jeanne Achterberg, a researcher at the University of Texas Health Science Center, told *Prevention* magazine that she and her husband have come to believe the mental and physical are so closely interwoven that the term *body-mind* more accurately describes us.

"It's impossible to separate the mind from the body," she said. "They're a whole. Every thought affects the body in some way, and every physical movement or change is accompanied by some mental alteration."

In a series of studies, Dr. Achterberg and her coworkers examined the personalities of approximately two hundred terminal cancer patients. They found a striking difference between those who significantly outlived their predicted life expectancies and those who did not. The survivors shared a whole host of positive psychological traits—things like an utter refusal to give up hope, a rejection of their role as invalids, and openness to new ideas and a powerful belief in themselves.

"These people refused to accept their sickness," Dr. Achterberg said. "I don't think they understood their 'limits.' They were what we call the 'superstars.'" She said that scientists suspect that chemicals called endorphins, the natural substances the body produces to soothe pain and stimulate the immune system, are released into the body from positive thinking.[1]

Many people know the story of Norman Cousins, a former editor of *Saturday Review*, who fought off a degenerative spinal disease with vitamin C and massive doses of laughter from watching old comedy movies.

Oil was also used in biblical times to crown the kings of Israel to ordain the priests of the temple. Each person who has accepted Christ as his personal Savior has been crowned as a member of God's Kingdom and ordained into his priesthood.

You are a prince or princess of the kingdom of the King of Kings and the Lord of Lords, not just any kingdom. Your value and your self-worth are beyond your wildest imagination, because you have the King of all Kings as your Father. Negative thinking denies your noble birthright.

Thousands of people in the United States have turned from negative thinking to possibility thinking. One of those people, a man named Terry Larson, now works for my father as manager for the Crystal Cathedral, a job that takes an abundant amount of possibility thinking to keep up with Dad's unusual ideas, such as flying thirteen angels from the top of the twelve-story pinnacles on each side of the Crystal Cathedral during the "Glory of Christmas" pageant.

Ten years ago, Terry Larson was so depressed he thought about suicide. His wife had breast cancer. Terry had just purchased a furniture business and didn't have family health insurance, so the grief of watching a loved one struggle with this dreaded illness was compounded by the pressure of the increasing medical expenses.

His nephew, Jim Coleman, who was working for the Schuller Ministries, called Terry one Saturday and said, "Uncle Terry, you ought to watch 'The Hour of Power,' tomorrow. Dr. Schuller is interviewing a guest you'll like."

Terry can no longer remember who the guest was or what he said, but Terry felt as if his testimony and my dad's sermon were meant just for him. The next Sunday

Terry wanted to listen to the program again. "Watching 'The Hour of Power,'" Terry says, "is like eating peanuts. Once you start, you can't stop."

In the next weeks Terry decided, "I'm going to try being positive." Instead of getting up in the morning and thinking his wife was going to die, he started thinking she would get better and that, somehow, over a period of time, he also would be able to pay the medical bills. He and his wife prayed together for her recovery. In the next month, she underwent surgery and the doctors reported, "We think the cancer has been totally removed."

In thanksgiving for her recovery, Terry and his wife decided to attend the Easter service at the Crystal Cathedral, which was only ten minutes from their house. The people they met were so friendly and they so enjoyed being a part of the congregation, they changed from TV churchgoers to members of the Crystal Cathedral congregation. During the next year Terry became more and more involved in volunteer work at the cathedral. When Rancho Capistrano needed to be developed, my dad decided Terry was the man for the job, since he had been a commercial and residential designer.

My dad's Possibility Thinker's Creed is: "When faced with a mountain, I will not quit! I will keep on striving until I climb over, find a pass through, tunnel underneath—or simply stay and turn the mountain into a gold mine, with God's help!"

Terry is the one person I know who has literally "moved mountains" for my dad. The roads leading into the ranch were too narrow for the traffic from Sunday morning services and renewal meetings. But the roads were set on hills and low-lying mountains. No one thought they could be moved. No one, that is, except Terry Larson. If he could overcome his fear of his wife's death and his own bankruptcy, what was a mountain to him? Child's play.

Faced with such "impossible tasks," Terry's motto has become, "The difficult takes a day, the impossible takes a little bit longer."

In the next weeks Terry and his men cut down a portion of the mountain and back-filled the remaining slopes so the soil would be compact and the earth would not slide. A black-topped road now leads into the ranch, which will easily accommodate two-lane traffic.

Terry says, "If you were to think negatively working for Dr. Schuller, you would never be able to accomplish the things he wants done. The first step is to get excited, and when Dr. Schuller describes something to you there's no way you can keep from getting excited. Anyone who watches him knows what I mean.

"Rather than worrying about how I can do what he wants, I start thinking about how to make it even more spectacular than he's saying."

Once the major renovations to the ranch were completed, Dad appointed Terry Larson to be Cathedral Manager, which meant supervising all the work on the cathedral and its grounds and also supervising the lighting, sound, and staging for major events like the "Glory of Christmas" and the "Glory of Easter."

About two weeks before Thanksgiving in 1983, Dad told Terry he wanted the statue of Job, which was being created by sculptor Dallas Anderson, in place for Thanksgiving services. Terry and Dad flew to Utah to meet with Dallas, who promised the statue would be finished and delivered before Thanksgiving. "But you'll never be able to erect the granite and cement bases for the statue in such a short time," Dallas Anderson warned. "There's no way you can have the statue in place by Thanksgiving."

"Don't worry about that," my dad assured Dallas. "Terry can do the impossible.

On the plane back home, Terry and Dad redesigned the garden area in front of the arboretum, the former sanctuary of the Garden Grove Community Church, to accommodate the new statue. They decided to move the statue of the Good Shepherd to another area of the garden and to replace the cement block wall in front of the arboretum with a longer stone wall. Then they designed the first Walk of Faith (a pathway of marble plaques engraved with Scripture verses and the names of those who have contributed two thousand dollars to the ministry).

Terry had two statues to move and two cement granite bases to build, one wall to tear down and another to build—plus a small pool to construct and a unique marble pathway to landscape with trees and flowers—all by Thanksgiving.

When Dad and Terry returned to the cathedral, they walked over to the garden between the Tower of Hope and the Cathedral to make the final decision about where the statue of Job should sit. Dad pointed to a grassy area and said, "This would be the perfect spot!"

Before Dad reached his office on the twelfth floor of the Tower of Hope, Terry's men had already dug the first hole and started putting the wooden frames into the ground for the cement.

Soon Dad glanced out the window and saw what Terry had done. He told his secretary, "If I ever get sick, don't tell Terry, because he'll certainly have me buried before I die."

Terry always uses his own staff to accomplish these miracles. "I couldn't do it without them," he says. "They're conditioned to immediate deadlines. The larger the challenge, the more excited we all get.

"They say that long-distance runners reach a particular euphoria. I believe our whole crew gets that, especially if we have huge projects that other people say can't be done. Our pleasure comes from seeing the amazed look on people's faces when it happens. We enjoy turning mountains into gold mines."

Each of us needs to claim his noble birthright, as Terry Larson has. We need to think positively. Yes, we can move mountains if we try.

Spiritual Health

The final promise of the verse, "You anoint my head with oil," is that God will heal our souls. Our subconscious mind lies beyond our conscious mind. Within this subconscious state lies the soul, which stores our pain and sorrow and our joy and happiness. The soul knows the magnitude of God himself, far beyond our own comprehension.

Because we have free will, it's easy for us to fight against the Will of God, even at this subconscious level. Actor Dean Jones knows this all too well. Before his wife's healing, Dean admits, "I was somewhere between an agnostic and an atheist."

Dean had "succeeded" in life without any help from God. The story of that success is every actor's dream. He came to Hollywood in 1955 after being discharged from the Naval Air Corps with only $430 in his pocket. He intended to stay just long enough to catch a plane for New York where he planned to pursue a singing career.

For fun, he decided to enter the Peter Potter Amateur Contest. He won two cases of Formula 9 Shonetex Shampoo, which he had trouble giving away on Sunset Boulevard at midnight one night, and a multi-colored plastic hassock, which rolled out of the trunk of his car somewhere between Hollywood and San Diego.

But these meager prizes inspired Dean to stay in Hollywood and become an actor. But the time he was thirty, he was making $50,000 a week; he had a gorgeous home and two Ferraris—everything he thought would satisfy him when he arrived in Hollywood with $430 in his pockets.

Even after his wife's healing, Dean still fought against God's will to be a part of his life. Then one evening in September of 1973 Dean was out of town, sitting alone in a motel room. He was tired and depressed about a life that he felt was completely meaningless. *There must be something more to life*, he thought.

He looked back on his past. He had tried everything to find happiness—fame, money, women, fast cars. Nothing had satisfied him. Then he remembered how inspired he had been as a child when his Sunday school teacher in Alabama told him the story of Jesus' birth. As he thought again about the story, he realized God's gift of his Son was meant as a personal gift for him.

He knelt by the bed and put out a wager to God. "If

you're real, I'll take you up on your promises. Show me that you exist."

No voice answered his request. Nothing changed. In desperation, Dean said, *All right. I'll give you my life.* It was then that he felt a peace and contentment that far surpassed any joy he had experienced as a successful actor. "It was like a rebirth," he says. "I've never been the same."

As Dean found out, God is always ready to heal our souls. It is never too late to receive new life and strength from him, whether we're twenty-five or ninety-five. God promises each of us that he will heal our souls.

We need to pray the prayer, "Lord, heal my soul—the very deepest core of my being. Heal the guilt I may be feeling and help me to want to do your will."

In the first few months of 1984 I thought God's will for me was to be celibate. One day in the spring of 1984 I was in my office preparing a sermon on Christ's famous Sermon on the Mount. The passage of Scripture that had been so difficult to reconcile with my divorce was part of this sermon.

Here Jesus gave the people a new teaching on divorce. Whereas Jewish law had allowed a man to divorce his wife for any reason as long as he gave her a certificate of divorce, Jesus said, "Whoever divorces his wife for any reason except sexual immorality causes her to commit adultery; and whoever marries a woman who is divorced commits adultery."[2]

I felt I had to come to grips with this passage before I could be at peace. I went to the floor-to-ceiling bookcases in my office and looked for the volume on Matthew in Barclay's Commentaries. Surely he could give me some insight into the Scripture. But the volume was missing.

In one of those coincidences (which are often not really coincidences at all) I had just unpacked my Great-uncle Henry's library, which he had willed to me only a few months earlier. I saw his commentaries by C. H. Lenski, a conservative theologian of the first half of the twentieth century. I had previously referred to his commentaries in my father's library and had felt his interpretation was often quite good, so I selected his commentary on Matthew.

Fifty years ago, Lenski had explained this passage better than anyone else. "There is no passive verb in Greek for the words, *to commit adultery,*" he said. "Scholars have wrongly translated these words in this passage as active verbs.

"Since our English fails us here," Lenski said, "we must express the two passive forms as best we can to bring out the passive sense of the Greek forms. We attempt this by translating the [words as an] infinitive: 'he brings about that she is stigmatized as adulterous,' and the finite verb: 'he is stigmatized as adulterous.'

"Nothing in the words of Jesus forbids such a woman (or, if the case is the reverse, such a man) to marry again," Lenski went on to say. "Such a prohibition is always presumed, but without the least warrant in Jesus' own words. It is this false presumption that caused the current mistranslations."[3]

I felt as if God was answering my question. I was not violating his will by desiring to have a wife. My father had told me this before. He had begun by sharing with me a dream of his.

"I saw two wedding rings, intertwined as they often are on wedding invitations and announcements. Then one wedding ring broke away, saying, 'I don't want to be married.' The bond was broken, and there was nothing the other ring could do about it.

"Marriage," Dad said, "takes two who want a relationship, two who want to be married. There was nothing you could do about it, Robert. You do not have to feel guilty. I believe God would want you to remarry."

I felt as if God was erasing any remaining guilt I felt by bringing these two thoughts together. I knew he had forgiven any mistakes I had made.

Pray the prayer, "Heal me, Lord." Expect God to heal your mind, your body, and your soul. Then watch for him to work in your life.

David suggests that you will not only be filled with happiness, you will be bursting with it. The verse, "You anoint my head with oil," ends with the joyful statement, "My cup runs over." Ordinary people, just like us, can move mountains—with God's help!

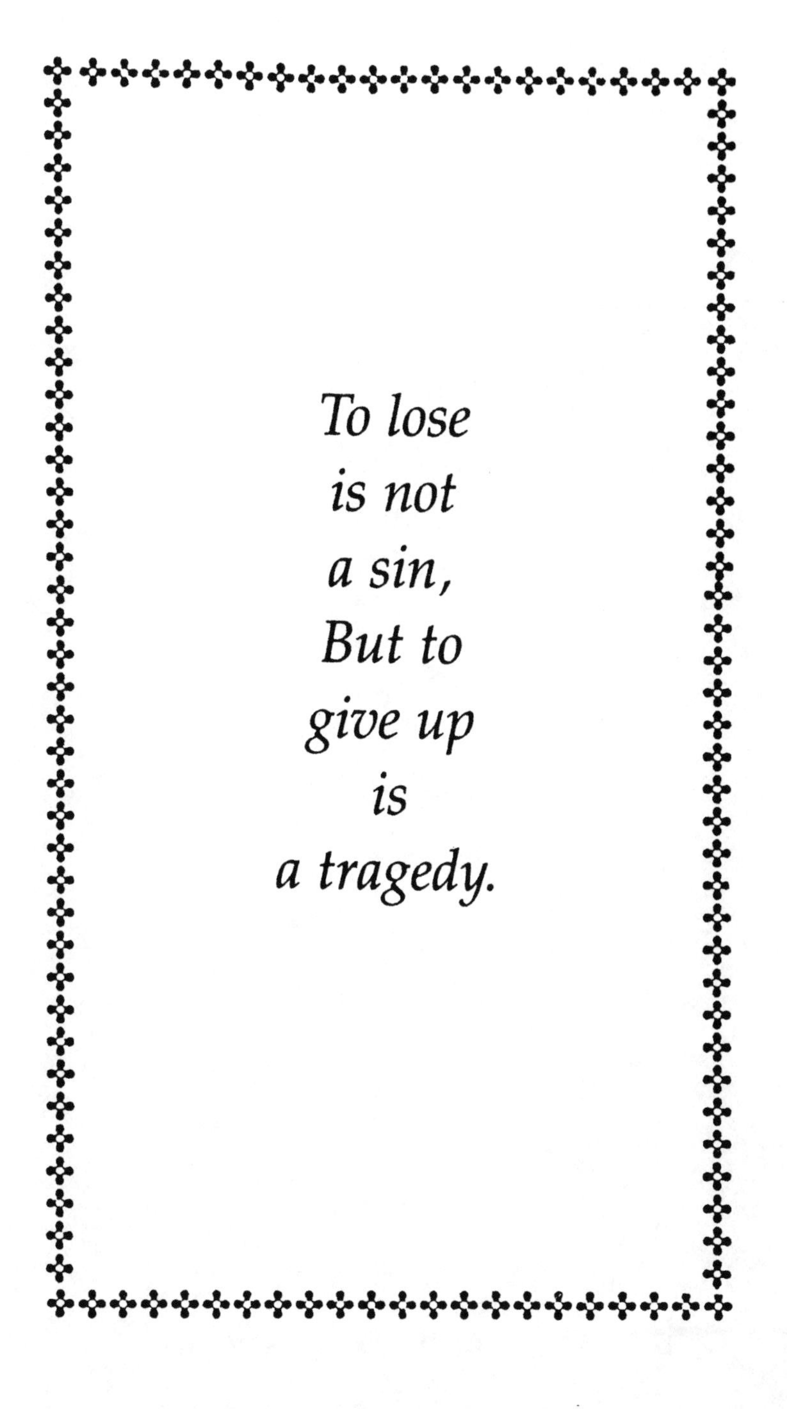

To lose
is not
a sin,
But to
give up
is
a tragedy.

STEP TEN

✣ ✣ ✣

Prepare Yourself for Lifelong Fulfillment.

"Surely goodness and mercy shall follow me all the days of my life. And I will dwell in the house of the Lord forever."

Not long ago I was interviewing Jim Jantz, a successful Canadian businessman, for "The Hour of Power" broadcast. After Jim shared his testimony, I asked, "What happened to you after you made Christ the center of your life?"

Jim looked at me squarely and answered very frankly, "Actually, I was still faced with all the problems I had been facing before I was a Christian. The problems didn't go away."

Jim's answer stayed with me. I spent several days studying conversion experiences to see if his had been unique. What I discovered was that not only was Jim's situation not unique; for a fact, many people's problems *increased* after they became Christians.

I began to question my own circumstances. When I became a Christian did my problems disappear? No. What about you? Did your problems disappear when you became a Christian? No. Before you can take the final step in getting through the going-through stage, you must understand three realities of being a Christian. The first reality is this: *Problems don't go away just because we become Christians.*

Happiness Is a Decision

Maybe some of you have had an experience like this: you come home from the mountains after a weekend retreat and the first thing you see is the smog lying all over the basin. You groan, "Oh, I've gotta go back to that?"

And then you go to pick up the kids. You say, "Hi, Johnny, I'm home!" and little Johnny runs in the opposite direction.

You finally grab him and he says, "I don't want to go home."

You start to go and the babysitter says, "That will be fifty dollars," and gives you a look that says, "You're getting off cheap." Back to reality. You have to come down from the mountains to the problems of everyday life.

Sometimes you think, "Why in the world did I become a Christian? What good is it doing for me? It hasn't solved any of my problems."

Some people misunderstand Christianity. They think that because it's based on a belief in a supernatural God that it should have magical qualities about it. Some people believe that once they become Christians, there will automatically be a "presto-change-o" altering of their lives. Where they formerly had worries and problems, they expect blissful contentment.

This is not only non-Scriptural, it is naive. The second reality of living the Christian life is this: *Being Christians does not mean we are always going to be happy.*

Consider Paul, for example. When he was blinded on the road to Damascus, he accepted Jesus Christ as his personal Savior and then tried to live a new life. But no one trusted him. When the Jews found out he had become a Christian, they branded him a traitor and turned against him. When he turned to the Christians, they felt he was trying to trick them; so, they also rejected him. When he tried to preach as an independent evangelist, he was arrested by the Romans and sent to jail in Rome—all because he had accepted Christianity.

Happiness is not a state of being. It's a state of consciousness. I realized this one day when I was driving down the freeway and saw a bumper sticker that said, "Happiness is being single." A little while later I saw another car with a bumper sticker that said, "Happiness is being married." Since I'd been happy when I was single and happy when I was married, I realized happiness isn't a matter of "being" anything. It's a conscious *decision* we make. Personal happiness is something each of us is responsible for on a day-to-day basis. Let me tell you how I learned this.

When I was growing up, mornings were the hectic time of our family life. My mother would come running through the house and wake everyone up at seven o'clock. At ten minutes after seven, she'd race through the house again and wake everybody up again. Then she'd go to the kitchen and start making breakfast. Each of us had chores to do. My sisters set the table and made the beds. They probably had other chores, but I've forgotten them. I've never forgotten my own routine, however. I'd bring in the milk. Then I'd walk the dog, sweep the walks, and take out the trash. Every morning for years I did those four things.

At exactly five minutes before eight, everyone had to be at the breakfast table ready to eat. By eight o'clock the food was gone. That gave us five minutes for a short devotion. My father would say a few comments, we'd read some Scripture, and then we'd always end with this motto: "I'm going to be happy today, though the skies may be cloudy or gray. No matter what comes my way, I'm going to be happy today." That determination set the tone for the day.

I suggest that you also begin your day with a similar mindset. That doesn't mean you're going to be spared from your problems. It doesn't mean you're always going to conquer the sorrow you'll feel. Sorrow is very real; problems are very real.

One of the ironies of life is that sometimes our greatest sorrows can come right on the heels of our greatest experiences of joy and serenity. This happened to me in July, 1978. I was in London on my way home after leading a tour group to Israel. We had seen the Mount of Beatitudes and walked in the Holy Land. I had felt very close to God those days.

During our stopover in London I was summoned to the office of the hotel manager and told that the British booking agency I had secured rooms with had gone bankrupt. The agency's check for our room fees had bounced. The manager insisted that I immediately pay him $4,568.

"You've got to be kidding. That's a lot of money. I don't have that much cash with me. Will you take a personal check?" I asked.

"No!" he replied emphatically. "But I will take cash and a credit card."

I gave the manager what cash I could spare and he drew the rest against my American Express credit card. Wow, was I broke?

But it got worse. When I returned to my room, I received a trans-oceanic call from my sister Sheila. She gave me the news that my sister Carol had been in a motorcycle accident and that Carol's leg had been amputated.

There was no way I could just laugh away these problems. I was a Christian, but I was not feeling happiness every moment of my life. Sorrow is a very real emotion. Our feelings of sorrow and depression don't go away. Life continues as normal—but with a difference. We can face our problems with faith.

A third reality about the Christian life is this: *Becoming Christians changes our lives because it enables us to face our problems with faith.*

Christianity does not make you a better person than your neighbor. Christianity makes you a better person than you would be if you were not a Christian. Christianity builds faith. Christianity gives you a positive attitude. Christ purifies you and prepares you to meet your maker.

We have our imperfections, but Jesus Christ came into this world so that you and I might be perfected through him and brought before the Father as a perfect creature through Jesus Christ. Our faith in him enables us to use that faith as a shield against life's challenges.

Using Our New Faith

I told you at the beginning of this book that my divorce from Linda and the separation from my two children was one of the greatest tests of my faith. I would now like to share with you how the strength of my faith not only led me through those challenging days, but also helped me regain custody of my son and daughter.

A few months after Linda left she asked if we could liquidate our assets so she could have her share of our home's equity in cash. I told her that a quick sale of our house would be unlikely, but I agreed to give her a five-figure cash advance against that sale. Linda used the money to invest in a condominium in Lake Forest and moved there with our children. Our divorce stated that we would have joint custody of our children, but no one was quite sure how to define that term. I felt it meant I had free access to the children, but Linda felt it restricted me to her schedule.

Prices are quite high in California and Linda soon exhausted her savings and was unable to keep the new condominium. She took the children and moved to Los Angeles. She also hired a new lawyer and petitioned me to increase alimony and child-support payments to more than we had previously agreed upon, more, in fact, than I could afford. The settlement of our divorce came to trial in November of 1984. Linda was awarded custody of the children, even though the family support was less than she had anticipated.

At this point, no one was happy. I was unhappy because my children had been moved so far away from me. Linda was unhappy because she did not think she had enough money to live on.

The closing line of the Twenty-third Psalm somehow seemed difficult for me to believe during this period. It promised that I would experience "goodness" and that God would show "mercy" toward me, but instead I felt overwhelmed and puzzled.

My friend Chuck Todd, an attorney, knew how both Linda and I felt. He contacted Linda and suggested there might be room for new negotiations. "Let's meet at a local restaurant to talk about it," he urged.

On the day of the meeting Linda arrived very early. Chuck came somewhat early, too, and they began to discuss Linda's needs. Although Chuck was representing me, he wanted to work out an agreement that would provide the most benefit to each member of the family. To my amazement, by the time I arrived at the restaurant, the negotiations were over. It was the Lord's perfect timing to have Chuck meet privately with Linda before I arrived.

The new settlement pleased everyone. Linda received a generous one-time payment, which enabled her to have enough money to live on, and at the same time relieved me from having to pay alimony and child support. Linda released the children into my custody but reserved the right to see them on weekends and to take them every other holiday. During the summers, the children would go to live with Linda but would spend weekends with me. In 1990 the process would reverse itself.

I experienced God's goodness and mercy.

New Challenges

Donna and I had only been married two months when the children moved in with us. A couple of weeks later we were given a full-grown springer spaniel by some friends who were moving into an apartment that didn't allow pets. The tranquil home we had known as newlyweds suddenly became a hot spot of constant activity.

A member of my congregation approached me and said, "Robert, seems to me you could use a housekeeper."

I shook my head. "It would be nice, but I don't know if we can afford it."

"Well, I know of a woman in northern California who is a refugee. She needs food and a place to live and you need a housekeeper. Seems like a good match to me."

Donna and I discussed it and we agreed to send for the woman. When she arrived, we discovered she couldn't speak English. (And she discovered we couldn't speak Spanish.) She was from El Salvador and had been allowed into this country after the revolution in 1981.

She has stayed with us since 1984 and has been very helpful, but during the first few weeks we really had to struggle with the language barrier.

In the midst of that adjustment, a new situation arose.

One afternoon Donna drove to school to pick up my daughter, Angie. The teacher motioned for Donna to park her car and to come to see her. Angie was at the teacher's side.

"You are Mrs. Schuller?" the teacher asked Donna as she walked up.

"Yes . . . yes, I am. Is anything wrong?"

"I'm afraid you and your husband have a lot of work ahead of you," said the teacher. "Angie cannot read or spell. She is two reading books behind the other first graders in my class. I can't help her on an individual basis because I have thirty students in my class this year."

Donna didn't quite know what to say. She knew that Angie wasn't dumb but she had attended three schools in less than a year, which was enough to confuse any child. "I'm sorry," Donna mumbled. "This is all new to me. We only took custody of Angie a few weeks ago."

"I'm sure it's difficult, but you'll have to get started right away nevertheless. I'll loan you these texts to help you." With that, the teacher handed several books to Donna.

We all faced the challenge. We worked individually with Angie, and she worked on her own. We all encouraged her, boosted her self-confidence, showed our faith in her. A year later she was awarded a Principal's Certificate for Scholastic Achievement. Again we experienced God's goodness and mercy.

Understanding Mercy

When David wrote the Twenty-third Psalm, he had no idea his reference to God's mercy would later play a major role in his own life. As great a man as David was, he was also as human as you or I. He failed like anyone else. He disappointed God and had to beg for his grace and mercy.

God was long-suffering, and he showed mercy on David. After David had committed adultery with Bathsheba and conspired to murder her husband, God sent Nathan to admonish David for his wickedness.

By using a metaphoric story, Nathan made David see himself for the man he had become. David loathed himself. He tore his clothes, dressed in sackcloth and ashes, and fell prostrate on the floor in prayerful humility before God.

For three days David cried and prayed and moaned and begged God for forgiveness. He would not eat, he would not drink water, he refused to talk to anyone. Hour after hour he prayed, day after day; on and on he pleaded for mercy, but God remained mute.

Finally, at the end of three days, David grasped the vision of who he was without God. There he was, the mighty general of the host and king of Israel, now reduced to a dirty, unshaven, cold, tired, hungry, thirsty beggar dressed in burlap and sprawled on a bare floor.

At that point David knew he deserved to lose his kingship and his position as military commander and even his life. He yielded himself completely to God and submitted his will to the Lord's. Whatever judgment God in his infinite wisdom deemed appropriate, David was ready to receive it.

It was then that God sent Nathan to tell David he could remain as king and general and that once again God would use him for great accomplishments. God's mercy was complete.

I have a friend who went through a similar experience, except that instead of three *days*, this man was given three *years* to grasp the vision of who he was without God.

It happened this way. After completing college, this young man had several thousands of dollars in school debts that he needed to repay. He was approached by someone who offered him a substantial amount of money if he would try to smuggle some illegal drugs out of Mexico and into California. In the process, he was arrested by the Mexican police and was sentenced to thirty-six months in prison.

The prison food was so bad the man suffered from dysentery and malnutrition. In winter he had no heat; in summer he sweltered. Life was a constant battle against lice, rats, flies, and cockroaches. Yet, ironically, today this man looks back on those miserable days as golden years.

"I had three years to think about what God was trying to teach me about how I had messed up my potential in life," he told me. "I used those three years to read books, one of which was the Bible, to learn to speak Spanish, and to master some trade skills. I left that prison a completely changed man."

It took three years for that man to get through his going-through stage. God's mercy was complete. Since then, he has had other going-through stages to endure, but he has done so with poise and confidence.

That's the way life is. We no sooner come out of one going-through stage than we enter another. We are just pilgrims. But those of us who know Christ as our Savior never walk alone. Whether we are confronted by bankruptcy, divorce, physical abuse, or spiritual turmoil, God can use our going-through stages to prepare us for greater things. Though he was a failure, David could pray, "Surely goodness and mercy shall follow me all the days of my life."

Dwelling in God's House

The final verse in the Twenty-third Psalm links David's thoughts of goodness to his thoughts of constant "residency" in God's family: "Surely goodness and mercy shall follow me all the days of my life, and I will dwell in the house of the Lord forever." David knew all the goodness the world had to offer would be worthless if he was not living in harmony with God.

As I studied this passage recently, I asked myself three pertinent questions:

- Who will dwell in the house of the Lord forever?
- Where do our joy and strength come from?
- When does forever begin?

There are many things in this world you cannot do unless you are qualified or privileged. For example, I can stand in my church's pulpit and preach the gospel, perform marriage ceremonies, conduct funerals, issue the sacraments, and coordinate the functions of operating a church because I am ordained and assigned to do these things. A layman does not have all of these privileges.

Conversely, I could apply for membership in the Royal Academy of Science, but my application probably would be rejected. I have not been trained as a scientist and have not made any great scientific discoveries. Hence, the door to admission in the Royal Academy is closed to me.

In 1983 a young man managed to sneak past the guards at Buckingham Palace and climb into a window of the queen's bedroom. When the queen came in to retire for the night, the man announced his presence and assured the queen he only wanted to talk to her. Guards were summoned and the man was arrested and placed in jail. The man had thought the queen would find it amusing that he had been able to sneak into her room. Instead he found out the palace was off-limits to commoners.

The exciting thing about the closing line of the Twenty-third Psalm is that the pronoun *I* can be replaced with your name or mine. We can read it, "And Robert A. Schuller will dwell in the house of the Lord forever" or "And John Smith... Mary Jones... (your name) will dwell in the house of the Lord forever."

Robert A. Schuller

Starting Your Forever

David said he would dwell with God *forever*. What did he mean by that? Does forever start on the day we pass from this life into everlasting life? Or does it begin before then?

The very instant we invite God into our hearts, our souls are secured by his grace for all eternity. Our everlasting lives transcend physical existence to spiritual existence. Paul laughed at the idea of death's being something to fear: "O, death, where is your sting?"

When I was ten years old, I used to hold a honeybee by its wings and then press it against a moist piece of cloth. The bee would alway sting the cloth and then I would remove its stinger. Later, I would let the bee crawl all over my arms and face and neck, and the girls at school would say, "Ohhhhhh!" They couldn't believe I was so brave. Of course, they didn't know that it's easy to be brave when you know there's no sting involved.

Christians who are eternally secure in Christ have a sense of security that lifts them above the worries of life and even above the fear of death. People who know where they are going can move with confidence and assurance. That's what makes Psalm 23 the key to getting through the going-through stage.

Each time I walk into our church sanctuary at Rancho Capistrano Community Church, I pause a moment to look at the stained-glass windows depicting the Good Shepherd and his sheep. My mind goes back to earlier times—the day John Crean turned down my request for land . . . the day our church was denied the college gym for services . . . the rainy season that threatened to cancel our services . . . the morning I had to announce my divorce to the congregation—and I'm reminded that in each of these "going-through stages" the Good Shepherd cared for me. He guided me through even the roughest of times.

The strength of the message of the Twenty-third Psalm is that we Christians know where we're going. Our faith can lead us out of the valley into the Promised Land. Our forever begins today and lasts forever!

Happiness
is not
a state of being.

It is a state
of consciousness
that creates our
state of being.

Notes

Getting through the Going-through Stage

1. 1 Timothy 3:2-5.
2. Matthew 19:9.

Step 1

1. 1 John 1:9
2. Deuteronomy 32:7,9-10,12.
3. 1 Samuel 17:37.
4. 1 Samuel 16:7.

Step 2

1. Luke 18:1.
2. Deuteronomy 24:1-4.
3. Luke 18:4.
4. 1 Chronicles 4:10.
5. Matthew 28:19.

Step 3

1. John 3:16.
2. James Hassett, "But That Would Be Wrong..." *Psychology Today*, November 1981, pp. 34-49.
3. Corrie ten Boom, *The Hiding Place* (Old Tappan, NJ: Revell, 1971), p. 217.
4. Revelation 2:7.
5. John 14:26.
6. Romans 8:26.

Step 4

1. 2 Samuel 12:13.
2. 2 Chronicles 7:14.
3. Ephesians 6:5, NIV.
4. Psalm 19:14.

Step 5

1. 1 Samuel 17:11.
2. 1 Samuel 17:33.
3. 1 Samuel 17:37.
4. Isaiah 40:31.

Step 6

1. Sam Justice, "Clergy Divorce: A Perplexing Problem." *Ministries*, Winter 1985/86, p. 24.

Step 7

1. Matthew 10:21.

Step 8

1. Romans 8:37.
2. Romans 8:31.
3. Romans 8:28.

Step 9

1. Stefan Bechtel, "Are You a Positive Person?" *Prevention*, vol. 36, (January 1984), pp. 38-39.
2. Matthew 5:32.
3. C. H. Lenski, *Matthew: The Commentaries of C. H. Lenski* (Columbus, Ohio: Lutheran Book Concern, 1934), p. 227.

About the Author

Reverend Robert Anthony Schuller is the founding pastor of Rancho Capistrano Community Church, one of the fastest growing churches in southern California. Born in 1954 in Blue Island, Illinois, he was virtually raised in the back of the family car in Garden Grove, California. There his mother served as volunteer organist and his father conducted church services on the snack bar's roof of a drive-in theatre, beginning what would become the Garden Grove Community Church and later the Crystal Cathedral of the Reformed Church of America.

Growing up under the influence of his famous father, Dr. Robert H. Schuller, Reverend Schuller naturally aspired at an early age to follow him into the Christian ministry. Young Robert entered Hope College in Holland, Michigan, and received his Bachelor of Arts Degree in Classics in 1976. He then returned to California to study at Fuller Theological Seminary while interning at the church in Garden Grove. During those years he took part in planning the Crystal Cathedral, oversaw the church's Home Bible Fellowship Program, and assisted his father on the internationally televised "Hour of Power."

After receiving his Master of Divinity Degree, he was ordained into the Reformed Church in America (the oldest protestant denomination with a continuous ministry in the United States since 1682). He was installed as Minister of Evangelism at the newly completed Crystal Cathedral, preparing to be groomed to succeed his father.

Only one year later, however, he felt led to pursue a different dream. His vision was to found a new church and human resource center in southern Orange County, California, that would minister to the whole person—body, mind, and spirit.

On November 1, 1981, services were first conducted at the Rancho Capistrano Community Church, the flagship of the Robert Schuller Renewal Ministries.

Reverend Schuller is regularly seen around the world on the "Hour of Power," the most widely watched of all televised ministries. He is also a member of the international board of directors of the Robert Schuller Ministries and president of the Robert Schuller Renewal Centers.

In addition to extensive travel in the United States, Reverend Schuller's speaking engagements have taken him to Europe, Africa, the Middle East, the Far East, Asia, Red China, Russia, Australia, Indonesia, South America, Central America, and Canada. His hobbies include various aquatic sports, running, weightlifting, racquetball, skiing, and big game fishing. In addition to the book *Getting through the Going-through Stage*, Robert has written *Life Changers, How to Be an Extraordinary Person in an Ordinary World,* and *Power to Grow beyond Yourself*.

Reverend Schuller and his wife, Donna, reside in San Juan Capistrano, with their children, Bobbie, Angie, and Christina.

Printed in the United States
by Baker & Taylor Publisher Services